THE
KITCHEN
PANTRY
COOKBOOK

For my dad, who always loved my cooking.

For my mom, who showed me that you are never too old to follow your dreams.

And for my husband, who made it possible for me to do the things I love.

Thank you. I love you all.

First published in the United States of America in 2013 by
Quarry Books, a member of
Quayside Publishing Group
100 Cummings Center
Suite 406-L
Beverly, Massachusetts 01915-6101
Telephone: (978) 282-9590
Fax: (978) 283-2742
www.quarrybooks.com
Visit www.QuarrySPOON.com and help us celebrate food and culture
one spoonful at a time!

10 9 8 7 6 5 4 3 2 1

ISBN: 978-1-59253-843-0

Digital edition published in 2013
eISBN: 978-1-61058-776-1

Library of Congress Cataloging-in-Publication Data is available

Design: John Foster at badpeoplegoodthings.com
Photography: Rina Jordan, with the exception of page 19, Erin Coopey
Food styling: Malina Lopez

Printed in China

THE KITCHEN PANTRY COOKBOOK

MAKE YOUR OWN
CONDIMENTS
AND ESSENTIALS

by Erin Coopey

Quarry Books
100 Cummings Center, Suite 406L
Beverly, MA 01915

quarrybooks.com

CONTENTS

CHAPTER FOUR: *Stocks*

CHAPTER FIVE: *Relishes and Refrigerator Pickles*

CHAPTER SIX: *Chips, Dips, and Dunks*

INTRODUCTION

Do you ever think about that jar of mayonnaise in your refrigerator? You know the one. It's been on a shelf for a month or so. Most people would think nothing of pulling it out to make a sandwich over the course of several weeks or even months, right? Hold on a minute, isn't mayonnaise made from egg yolks? Would you eat eggs that had spent a couple of months in your refrigerator? Probably not. So why is the mayonnaise okay? Let me put it another way: if I make something from scratch and it's only safe to eat for three to five days, why is it "okay" to eat a commercially made version of the same food after months on the shelf or in the refrigerator? The short answer is: it's not.

I think we take so much of the food we eat for granted. Now, I am not suggesting that all commercially made foods are evil, but let's face it, food production is a business. What is the goal of most businesses? To make money. How do you make money? By cutting costs—using GMO (genetically modified organism) food that grows faster but offers fewer nutrients, substituting cheaper ingredients such as corn syrup instead of natural cane sugar, and stretching foods with fillers made from starches and grain.

About ten years ago, I discovered that I was gluten sensitive. As a matter of fact, I'm sensitive to all grains. (I know. I won the lottery on that one, especially because I'm a chef.) That discovery forced me to take a hard look at the food I was eating, read labels, and even call companies for accurate information about vague terms like "modified food starch." I was really surprised at what I discovered. Most commercially produced foods are filled with an assortment of food starches, not to mention fillers, dyes, preservatives, gums and stabilizers, sodium, and sugars. I found I couldn't eat many of the products that I had in the past.

It probably wouldn't occur to most people to make the common items in the refrigerator or pantry. Why bother making ketchup or mustard from scratch? Well, first, you know what's actually in them. Second, the homemade versions taste better. Really! Try a sumptuous spoonful of creamy, eggy homemade mayonnaise and you'll balk at the artificial sweetness and salty, bland flavor of the commercial stuff.

With the onslaught of food allergies and sensitivities, autoimmune disorders, and obesity and the landslide of diseases that accompany it, I don't think any of us can take for granted what goes into our food. You may have heard the term "clean food" being used by national health experts such as Dr. Oz. Clean foods, according to Gerald Celente, director of the Trends Research Institute, are "foods free of artificial preservatives, coloring, irradiation, synthetic pesticides, fungicides, ripening agents, fumigants, drug residues and growth hormones."

With people's increased interest in how our food is produced and what goes into it, I think this book is timelier than ever. For me, it's not about giving up the things you love. It's about gaining the knowledge to make delicious food yourself, experimenting, and having fun. I get a kick out of making something from scratch that most people wouldn't have thought of trying. I'm thrilled to find how easy it is to do and how amazing the results are, and I love the surprised and excited reaction I get from friends and family. I know you'll love it, too.

So, whether you know someone with dietary restrictions or you simply want to control the quality of the food that you eat, *The Kitchen Pantry Cookbook* will show you how easy it is to make delicious, quality food in your own kitchen.

— Chef Erin

CHAPTER ONE: CONDIMENTS

"CONDIMENTS ARE LIKE OLD FRIENDS—HIGHLY THOUGHT OF, BUT OFTEN TAKEN FOR GRANTED."

— *Marilyn Kaytor, American food writer*

It's easy to take condiments for granted. Other than perhaps selecting a favorite brand, you may not think much about them. However, condiments play a role in our daily lives. Let's imagine a hamburger without ketchup, a hotdog without mustard, a rack of ribs without some delicious barbecue sauce. Boring, right?

Now that you are thinking about condiments, why not try making them from scratch? You might never have thought of making them yourself because we're so used to grabbing a jar or bottle from the grocery store shelves. A friend once asked, "Can you actually make mustard at home?" Well, the answer is yes! You can make mustard, mayonnaise, tartar sauce, ketchup, and more. And you're about to find out how. Most are surprisingly simple and downright, deliciously fun!

MAYONNAISE

Watching eggs and oil swirl together into mayonnaise seems almost like a magic trick, and it's ready in flash!

Yield: 1 cup (225 g)

Ingredients

2 raw egg yolks, from the freshest eggs you can find, at room temperature *(see page 12)*

½ teaspoon coarse sea salt or kosher salt

½ teaspoon mustard powder or Dijon mustard *(see page 29)*

1 teaspoon lemon juice

1 tablespoon (15 ml) white wine vinegar or cider vinegar *(see Note)*

1 cup (235 ml) oil

Pinch of sugar *(optional)*

Directions

Place the egg yolks in a blender or mini food processor. (Because this recipe only makes 1 cup [225 g], a full-size food processor may be too big to aerate the eggs properly. I find the bowl size of my mini prep to be perfect.) You can also whisk the mixture by hand. Process or whisk the egg yolks until they are light yellow and frothy. Add the salt, mustard powder, lemon juice, and vinegar and process/whisk until blended.

With the motor running (or whisking vigorously), slowly drizzle in the oil in a very light, steady stream. Don't stop until you have added the entire cup. When all the oil is blended, stop the motor (or take a breath), open the bowl, and taste. Add more salt and sugar, if desired.

Serve after 1 hour or refrigerate for up to 3 days.

Have you ever taken a close look at your food processor? Does yours have a pencil lead–size hole or two in the top? Ever wonder what that was for? Well, it allows you to slowly stream liquid into whatever you are mixing. In this case, it is ideal for blending oil into mayonnaise. If you don't notice a hole, not to worry. You can accomplish the same goal with a slow, steady hand.

Note: Homemade wine vinegar *(see page 70)* or high-quality (Orléans Method) bottled vinegar is best for making mayonnaise. Some commercial vinegars are too acidic and may cause your eggs to partially coagulate rather than create a thick, creamy sauce.

Mayonnaise can be made with any variety of oils, from canola to flaxseed or olive oil. Experiment to decide which oil is your favorite. You can even try infused oils like red pepper or basil to change the flavor. Be creative! Here are some other variations you might like to try:

Chipotle Mayonnaise—Add 1 teaspoon adobo sauce from a jar of chipotles en adobo to the finished mayonnaise. You get all the flavor without all the heat.

Piquant Mayonnaise—Add 1 teaspoon grated onion *(see page 18)* to the finished mayonnaise.

Curry Mayonnaise—Add 2 teaspoons mild curry powder when you add the mustard powder at the beginning of the recipe.

Tarragon Mayonnaise—Substitute tarragon vinegar for white wine vinegar/cider vinegar and add 1 tablespoon (4 g) minced fresh tarragon to the finished mayonnaise.

Harissa Mayonnaise—Harissa is a North African condiment made from hot chiles. You can find it online or in specialty stores. Add 1 tablespoon (14 g) to your finished mayonnaise and stir to combine. It makes a great spread for turkey and Havarti cheese sandwiches.

How to Choose Your Eggs

When making sauces like aioli or mayonnaise, you will be using raw eggs. (As a matter of fact, we should add the legal caveat here—"Consuming raw or undercooked meats, poultry, seafood, shellfish, or eggs may increase your risk of food-borne illness.") So, clearly you should choose the freshest eggs you can find from a reliable source. I am lucky enough to have a friend who raises chickens living around the corner. If you don't have your own urban farmer, try your local farmers' market or food cooperative.

If you are uncertain about the freshness of the eggs in your local market, you can also purchase pasteurized eggs. A pasteurized egg is an egg that has been gently heated in its shell to kill salmonella and other bacteria.

You can also coddle your eggs prior to using them in your sauce. Coddling refers to dipping the egg into water that is just under the boiling point. Simply heat a pan of water to the point that it is simmering rapidly. Gently lower your egg into the water with a slotted spoon. Allow it to sit for 90 seconds and then remove. This helps eliminate bacteria as well.

When you are preparing your mayonnaise or aioli, make sure your eggs are at room temperature prior to mixing. If both your eggs and your oil are at room temperature, you should have no trouble creating a smooth, thick sauce. If the eggs are too cold, they may hang in the oil, giving the sauce a thready, oily consistency. So, take your eggs out of the refrigerator and place them on the counter about 30 to 45 minutes prior to making your sauce.

BACON MAYONNAISE

Everything tastes better with bacon—even mayonnaise.
Bump up your BLT with this smoky, rich mayo. Try it on
a turkey sandwich or in potato salad.

Yield: 1 cup (225 g)

Ingredients

1 pound (455 g) bacon, your favorite type

½ cup (120 ml) water

Canola oil or safflower oil, as needed

2 raw egg yolks, from the freshest
  eggs you can find, at room
  temperature *(see page 12)*

½ teaspoon dry mustard
  or Dijon mustard *(see page 29)*

2 tablespoons (28 ml) white wine vinegar
  or lemon juice *(see Note)*

Coarse sea salt or kosher salt, to taste

Directions

Coarsely chop the bacon into 1-inch
(2.5 cm) pieces. Place the chopped bacon
in a medium-size saucepan. Add the water
and bring to a boil over medium-high heat.
Reduce the heat to medium-low and simmer
slowly, stirring occasionally, for 45 minutes
or until the fat is fully rendered.

Place a fine-mesh sieve over a mixing
bowl. Strain the bacon, pressing gently
on the bacon pieces to express as much

of the fat as possible. Pour the strained
bacon fat into a measuring cup. If the
drippings do not equal 1 cup (235 ml),
add canola oil or safflower oil to make up
the difference. If the drippings are more
than 1 cup (235 ml), pour off the excess
and store in the refrigerator to use for
sautéing potatoes or meats.

Place the egg yolks in a blender or food
processor. Process until light yellow. Add
the dry mustard and vinegar and process
until blended.

With the motor running, slowly drizzle in
the bacon fat. Don't stop until you have
added the entire cup. When all the fat is
blended, stop the motor, open the bowl,
and taste. Season with salt, if desired.

Serve after 1 hour or refrigerate for up
to 3 days.

Note: Homemade wine vinegar *(see page 70)*
or high-quality (Orléans Method)
bottled vinegar is best. If your vinegar
is too acidic, it may cause your eggs
to partially coagulate rather than create
a thick, creamy sauce.

How to Mince Parsley

Grasp the parsley bunch by the stems with one hand and turn the bunch upside down so that the leaves are hanging over your cutting board. Using a sharp chef's knife, gently shave the leaves from the stems by drawing the blade downward toward the cutting board. Turn the bunch so that you can reach all the leaves. When you've trimmed away most of the leaves, set the stems aside.

Pick through the leaves to remove any large stems you may have trimmed from the bunch. Again using your chef's knife, begin to mince the parsley by rocking the blade back and forth over the leaves. To maintain control, place your fingertips of your non-cutting hand on the spine of the knife at the tip of the blade. This will help you keep your blade on the cutting board and enable a smooth rocking action as you chop.

Stop chopping from time to time to regroup the parsley, moving the leaves back into a pile by scraping the spine of your knife (not the sharp side) across your cutting board. Continue chopping until you have finely minced leaves.

Scoop the leaves off your cutting board into a clean kitchen towel using your hands or the spine of your knife. Gather the edges of your towel up to form a bundle. Rinse the bundled parsley under cold water, squeezing gently for 3 to 5 minutes. You'll notice the water that runs out of the towel will become lighter green as you rinse. (By the way, don't worry about staining your towel. The parsley will wash away when you launder it as you normally do.) When the water running through the towel becomes almost clear, stop and wring the bundle to remove as much excess water as possible. Open the bundle and you should have clean, fluffy, ready-to-use parsley.

HERBED MAYONNAISE

This is great for chicken or shrimp salad, or with poached salmon or chilled ahi tuna steaks.

Yield: About 1 1/3 cups (300 g)

Ingredients

1 cup (225 g) freshly made
   mayonnaise *(see page 10)*

1 tablespoon (4 g) minced parsley *(see sidebar)*

1 tablespoon (3 g) minced chives

1 tablespoon (4 g) minced tarragon

1 tablespoon (15 g) sweet pickle relish

1 tablespoon (9 g) minced red bell
   pepper *(see page 121)*

1 tablespoon (9 g) minced
   hard-boiled egg *(optional)*

Directions

Combine all the ingredients in a small mixing bowl. Stir until well blended. Chill until ready to use. Store in the refrigerator for up to 2 days.

AIOLI or ALLIOLI

Aioli is a garlicky mayonnaise-style sauce common to the Mediterranean region. It makes a delightful dip for vegetables, particularly artichokes and asparagus. It's also commonly served with dishes like the Spanish tortilla de papas.

Yield: 1 cup (225 g)

Ingredients

1/2 teaspoon garlic puree *(see sidebar)*

1 small egg, the freshest you can find, at room temperature *(see page 12)*

1 teaspoon sherry vinegar or lemon juice

1 cup (235 ml) extra virgin olive oil

1/4 teaspoon coarse sea salt or kosher salt, or to taste

Directions

Place the garlic, egg, and vinegar in a small mixing bowl and whisk until thoroughly combined. Or alternatively, place the garlic, egg, and vinegar in a blender or food processor and whip until thoroughly combined.

Next, while whisking by hand or whipping in a blender or food processor, begin to very slowly add the oil. Try to pour in a very slow, steady stream so that the oil has time to emulsify with the egg. The mixture will start to thicken and become a pale yellow. When you've achieved the desired thickness, stop adding oil. Season with salt and serve.

How to Make Garlic Purée

Peel a clove of garlic. Slice off the dried stem end. Mince the garlic as finely as you can. Gather the minced garlic into a small pile. Sprinkle the garlic with a generous pinch of coarse sea salt or kosher salt. Lay your knife blade flat on your cutting board over the pile of garlic. Using the heel of your hand, press down on the knife and smear the garlic away from you across the cutting board. Use the spine of your knife to scrape the garlic back into a pile. Lay your knife flat on the pile and press and smear again. Repeat until the garlic has been mashed into a fine paste.

TARTAR SAUCE

Commercial tartar sauce is often full of sugar and corn syrup. This tangy tartar will add zip to your fish.

Yield: About 1 1/3 cups (300 g)

Ingredients

1 cup (225 g) homemade
    mayonnaise *(see page 10)*

2 tablespoons (30 g) minced dill pickle

2 tablespoons (18 g) capers,
    rinsed and chopped *(optional)*

1 tablespoon (4 g) minced
    fresh parsley *(see page 14)*

1 tablespoon (15 ml) lemon juice

1 teaspoon grated onion *(see sidebar)*

Directions

Mix all the ingredients together in a small mixing bowl. Chill until ready to use. Store in the refrigerator for up to 1 week.

Grated Onion

Grated onion is a wonderful way to add flavor to homemade sauces, dressings, and dips. I first learned about using grated onion from my friend and former instructor, Jean-Marie Rigolet, of the Bohemian Club. Jean-Marie told me his secret to good coleslaw dressing was just a little bit of grated onion. People don't even know it's in there, but it really enhances the flavor.

Grating an onion is as simple as it sounds. Simply peel the skin from an onion. Trim away the stem end, but leave the root intact. Hold the stem end of the onion against the fine side of a box grater/cheese grater and grate over a bowl. You may need to scoop the pulp off the inside of the grater with your fingertips.

You can store grated onion pulp, covered, in the refrigerator for up to 1 week. The flavor and pungency will diminish over time.

REMOULADE SAUCE

I used to frequent a restaurant in Northern California
that served grilled artichokes with remoulade sauce
that was to die for. This is my homage
to Bandera's remoulade.

Yield: About 1 1/4 cups (280 g)

Ingredients

1 cup (225 g) homemade mayonnaise *(see page 10)*

2 tablespoons (22 g) whole-grain
  mustard *(see page 27)*

2 tablespoons (6 g) minced chives
  or (12 g) scallions

1 tablespoon (15 ml) cider vinegar
  or tarragon vinegar

1 tablespoon (9 g) capers, rinsed
  and chopped

1 teaspoon anchovy paste

1 teaspoon minced fresh parsley *(see page 14)*
  or chervil

1 teaspoon minced fresh tarragon

1/4 teaspoon garlic purée *(see page 17)*

1 dash Tabasco sauce or cayenne pepper,
  or to taste

1 hard-boiled egg, finely chopped *(optional)*

Directions

Mix all the ingredients together in a small
mixing bowl. Chill until ready to use.
Store in the refrigerator for up to 3 days.

What Is Remoulade Sauce?

Remoulade is a French mayonnaise-based sauce, classically served with julienned celery root as a salad—Celeriac Remoulade. When it comes down to basics, you could say that remoulade sauce is, in essence, fancy tartar sauce. Both are mayonnaise based and usually include some sort of salty addition like pickle relish and a little acid like lemon juice or vinegar. However, remoulade is more flavorful than tartar sauce by far. It excites the palate with a variety of additions, including fresh herbs, mustard, and a little anchovy paste. (I know, anchovy paste … Let's try to be open-minded. Anchovy paste simply adds a little depth and saltiness to the sauce.)

Remoulade sauce is quite versatile as well. I mentioned how delicious it can be as a dipping sauce for artichokes, but like its cousin, tartar sauce, it's outstanding with fried fish and crab cakes. It makes a super dipping sauce for chilled shrimp, too, especially if you'd like to cut back on sugary cocktail sauce. It also makes a wonderful sauce for potato salad. In Belgium, it's served with french fries, and apparently they like it on hot dogs in Iceland.

In the South, remoulade takes on a whole different style—hot and spicy, like any self-respecting Cajun sauce. My version is a tip of the hat to a Creole style with whole-grain mustard and scallions or chives. You can try it with or without the hard-boiled egg. Both are tasty.

BALLPARK-STYLE YELLOW MUSTARD

This mustard is an American classic.

Yield: 1 cup (175 g)

Ingredients

1 cup (235 ml) water

3/4 cup (108 g) yellow mustard powder/dry mustard

3/4 teaspoon coarse sea salt or kosher salt

1/2 teaspoon turmeric

1 teaspoon garlic purée *(see page 17)* or 1/8 teaspoon garlic powder

1/8 teaspoon paprika

1/2 cup (120 ml) white distilled vinegar

Directions

Place the water, mustard powder, salt, turmeric, garlic, and paprika in a small nonreactive saucepan and whisk until smooth.

Cook the mixture over medium-low heat for 1 hour, stirring often. Whisk in the vinegar and continue to cook until the mustard has thickened to the desired consistency.

Allow the mustard to cool, transfer to an airtight container, and store in the refrigerator for up to 1 year.

Nonreactive vs. Reactive Cookware

Many of the recipes in this book specify using a nonreactive pan or bowl. Reactive cookware, meaning equipment made from aluminum or copper, can cause discoloration or impart a metallic, off taste in certain food. When a recipe suggests using nonreactive cookware, you can use glass, enamel, or stainless steel. If your pots and pans have an aluminum or copper core, that material is usually encased in a stainless steel shell, so they would be considered nonreactive as well.

SPICY BROWN MUSTARD

If you could describe mustard in the same way you describe wine, this one would be complex—spicy, tangy, sweet, and nutty, with exotic undertones.

Yield: 1 1/4 cups (220 g)

Ingredients

1/2 cup (120 ml) water

1 cup (112 g) crushed brown mustard seeds or 3/4 cup (132 g) whole brown mustard seed, finely ground *(see Note)*

1/2 cup (120 ml) red wine vinegar *(see page 70)*

1 teaspoon kosher or coarse sea salt

1/8 teaspoon ground cinnamon

1/8 teaspoon ground cloves

1/8 teaspoon ground nutmeg

1/8 teaspoon ground allspice

1/4 teaspoon black pepper *(optional)*

Directions

Combine all the ingredients in a glass or ceramic mixing bowl. Cover with plastic wrap and let sit at room temperature for 1 to 2 days so that the mustard begins to mellow and the flavors meld. Transfer to an airtight container. Cover and refrigerate overnight and use immediately or refrigerate for up to 6 months.

Note: I use pre-crushed brown mustard seeds from Penzeys Spices, but you can substitute whole mustard seeds. You will need to grind them into a fine powder using a food processor or spice mill prior to mixing them into the recipe. If you find that the final mustard still seems slightly watery after sitting at room temperature for 1 or 2 days, pour the mustard into a blender or food processor and process until smooth.

BAVARIAN-STYLE MUSTARD

This sweet-hot mustard is the perfect companion to wieners, bratwurst, and knockwurst. It also makes a nice dip for pretzels. I've suggested two different preparation methods—slow and quick—in this recipe. If you are interested in the natural mellowing of mustard and have the time, try the slow method. If you'd like to eat the mustard right away, the quick method is the one for you.

Yield: 1 cup (175 g)

Ingredients

1/2 cup (72 g) yellow mustard powder/dry mustard *(see Note)*

1/4 cup (60 ml) warm water

2 tablespoons (26 g) sugar

1 teaspoon kosher salt or coarse sea salt

2 tablespoons (28 ml) cider vinegar

Directions

Slow Method—Combine the mustard powder, warm water, sugar, and salt in a bowl. Stir until a smooth paste is formed. Cover the bowl with plastic wrap and let sit overnight or up to 24 hours.

Stir in the cider vinegar. Transfer the mustard to an airtight container. Cover. The mustard will continue to mellow if left at room temperature. You can allow the mustard to rest on your counter for up to 8 weeks before refrigerating. Test the flavor occasionally to determine whether it has mellowed to the level you desire. When you are satisfied with the flavor, transfer the jar to the refrigerator.

Quick Method—Increase the water to 1/2 cup (120 ml). Combine the mustard powder, warm water, sugar, and salt in a small saucepan. Heat over low heat for 1 hour or so, stirring occasionally. Maintain a low heat. Do not simmer or boil. Remove the pan from the heat and stir in the cider vinegar. Cool to room temperature and transfer to an airtight container. Cover and refrigerate. The mustard can be stored in the refrigerator for up to 12 months.

Note: For spicier mustard, try using Penzeys Regular Canadian Mustard Powder, a blend of brown and yellow mustard.

Heat and Mustard

I've seen many mustard recipes over the years that suggest mixing up the mustard, letting it rest overnight, and diving right in. I'm not suggesting those recipes are wrong, but—a word of warning—if you've mainly eaten commercially prepared mustards, you might be in for quite an assault on your taste buds, not to mention a clearing of your sinuses, and perhaps a flush of your tear ducts. Homemade mustard can take weeks to mellow.

So, why is the yellow mustard we buy from the grocery store less intense? Well, when mustard seeds are cracked or ground and mixed with cool liquid, a chemical reaction occurs that releases fiery chemical compounds, myrosin and sinigrin. Adding warm liquid instead diminishes some of the burst of heat. In addition, acids, like vinegar, can slow the decline of the heat. If you like a milder mustard, use warm water or warm the mustard over low heat and add the vinegar after the mustard has set for a time.

Incidentally, most mustard does not need to be refrigerated, but refrigeration does help maintain the potency.

CREAMY DILL MUSTARD

Dill and mustard are a classic pairing. Try serving this mustard with fish, especially salmon. It's also nice with shrimp, chicken, and pork.

For a unique potato salad dressing, mix 1/3 cup (58 g) Creamy Dill Mustard with 1 cup (225 g) mayonnaise *(page 10)*.

Yield: 2 cups (350 g)

Ingredients

1 1/2 cups (355 ml) water

1 cup (144 g) yellow mustard powder/dry mustard

1/2 teaspoon potato starch

1/4 teaspoon turmeric

Pinch of garlic powder

Pinch of paprika

6 tablespoons (90 ml) distilled white vinegar

1/4 cup (50 g) sugar

1 tablespoon (20 g) honey

2 teaspoons coarse sea salt or kosher salt

1 egg

4 teaspoons (20 ml) lemon juice

1/4 cup (60 ml) canola oil

2 tablespoons (8 g) minced fresh dillweed

1/4 teaspoon celery seed

Directions

In a small saucepan, combine the water, mustard powder, potato starch, turmeric, garlic powder, and paprika. Stir until a smooth paste is formed. Next add the vinegar, sugar, honey, and salt and stir to combine. Warm over medium-low heat, stirring constantly, until the sugar dissolves, about 10 minutes.

Next, whisk the egg and lemon juice in a small mixing bowl until light yellow. Slowly stream in the canola oil, whisking constantly. The egg mixture should continue to lighten in color and become frothy.

When the egg and oil are combined, whisk in 2 tablespoons (28 ml) of the warm mustard. When the mustard is completely incorporated, whisk in 2 more tablespoons (28 ml) of the warm mustard. Now that the egg mixture has been tempered, add it into the warming mustard a few spoonfuls at a time, stirring constantly.

When all the mustard is incorporated, stir in the dill and celery seed. This mustard makes a nice sauce when served warm. Refrigerate any unused portion for up to 3 days.

WHOLE-GRAIN MUSTARD

This recipe has a good kick because of the brown mustard seeds.
If you are a heat freak, add the horseradish, too!

Yield: 1 cup (175 g)

Ingredients

4 tablespoons (44 g) brown mustard seeds

2 tablespoons (22 g) yellow mustard seeds

1/2 cup (120 ml) white wine or water *(see Note)*

1 cup (235 ml) water

1/2 cup (72 g) yellow mustard powder

2 teaspoons coarse sea salt or kosher salt

1 1/2 teaspoons sugar

3 tablespoons (45 ml) wine vinegar
   or sherry vinegar

Directions

Place the mustard seeds and white wine in a small bowl. Cover and allow to rest for at least 8 hours or overnight.

Pour the mustard seeds and the wine into a small nonreactive saucepan. Whisk in the 1 cup (235 ml) water, mustard powder, salt, and sugar. When the mustard mixture is fully blended, slowly stir in the vinegar.

Heat the mustard over medium heat until it just begins to simmer. Reduce the heat to low and warm for 45 minutes, stirring occasionally. Remove the pan from the heat and allow to cool to room temperature.

Scrape the cooled mustard into a food processor and purée for about 30 seconds to 1 minute. The idea is to crush some, but not all, of the whole seeds.

Pour the puréed mustard into a glass jar and store in the refrigerator for up to 1 year.

Note: You can substitute a nice malty brown ale or stout for the wine/water in this recipe.

Variation: Horseradish Mustard—Stir in 2 tablespoons (16 g) grated fresh horseradish or prepared horseradish *(see page 38)* to the finished mustard.

Explore Sherry Vinegar

I bet you have a bottle of balsamic vinegar in your cupboard. I love a good balsamic, but I think we have become obsessed to the point that we've overlooked a world of exciting vinegars. Sherry vinegar is one you should check out. I recommend selecting a Vinagre de Jerez Reserva (reserve sherry vinegar from Jerez, Spain). A good reserve sherry vinegar is sweet, nutty, full-bodied, and acidic. For me, the flavor falls somewhere between balsamic and red wine vinegar—sweet yet lively. Try using some in your next vinaigrette (see page 76).

AUTHENTIC DIJON-STYLE MUSTARD

This mustard is rustic and coarse, a farm-style mustard common in the Burgundy region of France.

If you prefer a smoother version, try the Dijon Mustard on page 29.

Yield: 1/2 cup (90 g)

Ingredients

1/3 cup (59 g) black or brown mustard seeds

2/3 cup (160 ml) verjus *(see sidebar)*

Gray sea salt, to taste

Directions

Combine the mustard seeds and verjus in a small mixing bowl. Cover with plastic wrap and let rest at room temperature for 12 hours or overnight.

Remove the plastic wrap and scrape the mustard mixture into a food processor (or use a mortar and pestle if you prefer). Process or crush the seeds for several minutes until you have a slightly creamy blend that resembles a store-bought brown mustard.

Season with sea salt to taste. Typically, I usually add between 1/4 teaspoon and 1/2 teaspoon. Transfer the mustard to an airtight container. Cover and refrigerate for up to a year.

The Original Dijon Mustard

The original mustard of Dijon, France, is quite simple—a mixture of black mustard seeds, verjus, and salt. Although spicy-hot, it's not sharply tart like many bottled Dijon mustards. Verjus (pronounced vair-zhoo), from the French *verte* for green and *jus* for juice, is juice pressed from unripe, highly acidic grapes. The result is a delicately tart liquid that can be used in place of vinegar for salad dressings, sauces, and mustards. Because verjus lacks the bite-back acidity of vinegar, it's more palatable and therefore more wine-friendly. If you try substituting verjus in a homemade vinaigrette, increase the verjus by three times the amount of vinegar specified (e.g., 1 tablespoon [15 ml] vinegar equals 3 tablespoons [45 ml] verjus).

DIJON MUSTARD

I suggest using Penzeys Canadian Mustard Powder for your Dijon mustard because it's a blend of brown and yellow mustards that I think offers just the right amount of heat.

If you like hotter mustard, you could substitute Penzeys Oriental Canadian Mustard Powder, which is made from brown mustard seeds only.

Yield: 1 1/4 cups (220 g)

Ingredients

2 cups (475 ml) dry white wine

1 cup (160 g) chopped onion

3 cloves garlic, crushed

1 cup (144 g) Penzeys Regular Canadian Mustard Powder

1 tablespoon (20 g) honey

2 teaspoons coarse sea salt or kosher salt

1/2 cup (120 ml) cider vinegar

1/4 teaspoon citric acid *(optional)*

Directions

In a nonreactive saucepan, combine the wine, onion, and garlic; bring to a boil. Remove from the heat and steep for 5 minutes to infuse the flavors. Let cool and then remove the onion and garlic using a slotted spoon.

Add the mustard powder to the seasoned wine and whisk until smooth. Blend in the honey and salt. Return the saucepan to the stove top and heat the mustard slowly over low heat, stirring regularly, for 30 minutes. Add the vinegar and continue to heat for an additional 30 to 35 minutes until thickened. It's important to cook the mustard down very slowly to achieve the proper consistency. Don't rush the process or the mustard may have a granular texture. If it takes a little longer, that's okay. The finished mustard should be the consistency of jarred mustard. Remove from the heat and stir in the citric acid.

Pour the finished mustard into a glass jar to cool. Cover and let sit on the counter at room temperature overnight. Refrigerate for up to a year.

Variations: Honey Mustard—Add 1/4 cup (80 g) honey, or more to taste, to the finished mustard.

Tarragon Mustard—When adding the mustard powder to the seasoned wine, stir in 2 teaspoons dry tarragon leaves. Complete the recipe as directed.

KETCHUP

You'll think you're eating a national brand—minus the high-fructose corn syrup!

Yield: About 2 cups (480 g)

Ingredients

2 1/4 pounds (1 kg) plum tomatoes

1 1/2 cups (355 ml) distilled white vinegar

2 1/2 teaspoons coarse sea salt or kosher salt

1 cup (200 g) sugar

1 tablespoon (10 g) grated onion *(see page 18)* or 1 teaspoon onion powder

1/2 teaspoon mustard powder

1/4 teaspoon ground cinnamon

1/4 teaspoon ground cloves

1/4 teaspoon ground allspice

1/4 teaspoon ground black pepper

Directions

Bring a large pot of water to a boil. Add the tomatoes and blanch until the skins break and the flesh becomes soft, 5 to 10 minutes. Drain the tomatoes and press through a fine-mesh food mill or sieve to remove the skins and seeds.

Pour the sieved tomatoes into a medium-size saucepan. Add the vinegar and salt. Stir to combine. Bring the tomato mixture to a boil and then whisk in the sugar, onion, and spices. Return to a low boil, stirring occasionally, and cook until the mixture has reduced to one-fourth the original amount and has thickened, about 1 hour. Some tomatoes are more watery than others, so additional cooking might be necessary to reduce moisture. Your ketchup should be the consistency of tomato purée, slightly thinner than bottled ketchup. It will thicken slightly when it cools.

Pour into a sterilized jar *(see page 75)*. Cover and refrigerate. Store covered in the refrigerator for up to 1 month.

Food Mill vs. Food Processor

A food mill seems a little old-timey, doesn't it? In a world full of whirring, mechanized kitchen tools, using a hand-cranked device might not even occur to you. You might be tempted to simply throw your tomatoes into a food processor instead, but you'll get a very different outcome if you do. So what's the difference? A food mill separates the skins and seeds from the pulp, while a food processor chops and purées everything together. The biggest difference is texture; with a food mill you get a refined, smooth sauce, while a food processor turns out a slightly aerated, granular sauce. When it comes to ketchups, barbecue sauces, and fruit butters, you are better off using the food mill or a fine sieve.

Ketchup vs. Catsup

What's the difference? Well, as far as I can tell, there isn't actually a difference. I've read some accounts that suggest that catsup is spicier and ketchup is sweeter, but in researching recipes, that hasn't really borne out. I think it's simply a case of semantics.

Historians suggest that ketchup is derived from an Asian condiment ke-chiap or kêchap, made from pickled fish and spices. The sauce has morphed over the centuries. At its simplest, modern ketchup/catsup is a pickled fruit sauce. In my research, I've come across grape catsup, cucumber catsup, and banana ketchup, among others. Although tomatoes were brought to Europe from the New World in the mid 1500s, they weren't fully embraced until the 1800s, which, coincidentally, is when they started to become the primary ingredient in ketchup/catsup.

So why do we mainly see more ketchup than catsup on store shelves these days? Remember back in the 1980s when there was discussion at the USDA of classifying ketchup as a vegetable for school lunches? Rumor has it that the proposal specified "ketchup" rather than catsup. This specification apparently turned the tide on naming because companies tried to cash in on the school lunch market. Companies wouldn't want to supply catsup if ketchup was requested on the purchase order.

SWEET AND SPICY KETCHUP

I just love this ketchup. The cloves and cinnamon intensify the sweetness of the tomatoes, while the mustard and cayenne give it just a teensy kick. It makes me want to grill up a burger and sit in the sunshine!

Yield: About 2 cups (480 g)

Ingredients

2 1/4 pounds (1 kg) plum tomatoes

1 cup (235 ml) distilled white vinegar

1/2 cup (100 g) sugar

1/4 teaspoon cayenne pepper

1/4 teaspoon ground black pepper

1 teaspoon whole cloves

1 teaspoon mustard powder

1 teaspoon coarse sea salt or kosher salt

1 teaspoon ground cinnamon

Directions

Bring a large pot of water to a boil. Add the tomatoes and blanch until the skins break and the flesh becomes soft, about 5 to 10 minutes. Drain the tomatoes and press through a fine-mesh food mill or sieve to remove the skins and seeds.

Pour the sieved tomatoes into a medium-size saucepan. Add the vinegar, sugar, cayenne, black pepper, cloves, mustard powder, and salt; stir to combine. Bring the tomato mixture to a boil and then reduce the heat to medium. Simmer, stirring occasionally, until the mixture has reduced to one-fourth the original amount and has thickened, about 1 hour. If you find that your ketchup is still watery, continue to reduce it. Remember, the consistency should be like tomato purée—only slightly thinner than bottled ketchup. It will thicken a bit more when it cools.

Use a slotted spoon to remove the whole cloves. Stir in the cinnamon and refrigerate until cold. Store, covered, in the refrigerator for up to 1 month.

Plum Tomatoes

Most of my condiment and sauce recipes specify plum tomatoes—plum referring to the oblong or egg shape. The reason I suggest using plum tomatoes is that they have fewer seed pockets and are, therefore, meatier, with thicker fruit walls than slicing tomatoes such as beefsteak. Plum tomatoes are also referred to as sauce tomatoes or paste tomatoes. Look for varieties such as Roma, Italian, Italian Plum, and San Marzano.

KANSAS CITY–STYLE BARBECUE SAUCE

This barbecue sauce gets its natural smokiness from roasting tomatoes on the grill rather than using synthetic liquid smoke. It's gonna be your "go to" barbecue sauce!

Yield: About 2 cups (480 g)

Ingredients

2 cups (450 g) wood chips *(try applewood for sweeter smoke or hickory for bacon–like, smoky flavor)*

2 pounds (910 g) plum tomatoes

¼ cup (60 ml) canola or grapeseed oil

1 cup (235 ml) cider vinegar

1 cup (225 g) packed brown sugar

¼ cup (80 g) molasses

1 teaspoon coarse sea salt or kosher salt

¼ teaspoon ground black pepper

2 tablespoons (18 g) mustard powder

4 ½ teaspoons (15 g) grated onion *(see page 18)* or 1 ½ teaspoons onion powder

¼ teaspoon ground cloves

¼ teaspoon ground cinnamon

Pinch of cayenne, or more to taste *(optional)*

Directions

Immerse the wood chips in water and soak for 30 minutes.

Cut the tomatoes in half lengthwise, toss with the canola oil, and set aside.

Prepare a charcoal grill or preheat a gas grill to medium.

Drain the wood chips thoroughly. Tear two 12 x 18-inch (30 x 46 cm) sheets of heavy-duty aluminum foil. Divide the wood chips evenly between the two sheets.

Working with one sheet at a time, bring the 12-inch (30 cm) edges together and fold over several times to seal. Fold the remaining two sides to create a pouch with the wood chips inside. Use a paring knife to puncture the pouch about 7 to 10 times. Repeat with the remaining foil sheet.

Lay the pouches on top of the prepared coals or if using a gas grill, carefully lift the grill and place the pouches between two or three of the grill shields. When the wood chips begin to smoke, lay the tomatoes on the grill cut-side up. Close the grill cover and smoke for 20 minutes.

Transfer the grilled tomatoes to a food mill or sieve and press into a saucepan. Add the remaining ingredients. Mix well. Bring to a boil, reduce the heat, and simmer for 1 hour, stirring frequently.

Use immediately or transfer to a sterilized jar *(see page 75)*, cover, and refrigerate. Store in the refrigerator for up to 6 weeks.

CAROLINA-STYLE BARBECUE SAUCE

Carolina-style barbecue has a decidedly piquant flavor in comparison to its ketchup-based cousins. I love this sauce with grilled chicken, and it makes a mean pulled pork sauce. You can even use it as marinade before grilling.

Yield: 2 cups (480 g)

Ingredients

3/4 cup (130 g) Ballpark-Style Yellow Mustard *(see page 22)*

1/2 cup (100 g) granulated sugar

1/4 cup (60 g) packed brown sugar

1 cup (235 ml) cider vinegar

1/4 cup (60 ml) water

1 teaspoon hot paprika *(see Note)*

1/4 teaspoon red pepper flakes

1/4 teaspoon ground black pepper

3/4 teaspoon coarse sea salt or kosher salt

Directions

Mix all the ingredients in a medium-size saucepan. Stir to combine. Bring to a boil over high heat and then lower the heat and simmer for 10 minutes. The sauce can be used immediately or refrigerated for up to 1 month. If you plan to use this sauce as marinade, be sure to cool it in the refrigerator before adding the meat.

Note: For a lightly smoky flavor, you can substitute Spanish pimentón (smoked paprika). Look for picante, which means "hot." I love using pimentón to add a hint of smoke rather than using a synthetic liquid smoke.

CHILI SAUCE

I remember my mother buying bottles of Heinz Chili Sauce when I was a kid. We mainly used it to make cocktail sauce, but, I have to tell you, I think it's an underappreciated condiment. It's super on burgers, nice as a substitute for ketchup in Sloppy Joes, and great on pulled pork.

Yield: About 1 cup (275 g)

Ingredients

1 pound (455 g) ripe plum tomatoes

1/4 cup (40 g) finely chopped onion

4 1/2 teaspoons (14 g) finely minced chiles, such as ripe jalapeño or Fresno chiles

2 1/2 teaspoons firmly packed brown sugar

1/3 cup (80 ml) cider vinegar

1/2 teaspoon kosher salt or coarse sea salt

1/4 teaspoon celery seed

Directions

Bring a pot of water to a boil over high heat. Prepare an ice bath in a large bowl.

Core the tomatoes and then lightly score the bottom of each tomato with an X. Plunge the scored tomatoes into the boiling water for about 1 minute until the skins begin to crack along the X. Use a slotted spoon to remove the tomatoes from the boiling water. Lower the blanched tomatoes into a bowl of iced water.

Remove the chilled tomatoes from the water and peel away the skins using your fingers or a paring knife. Halve the tomatoes lengthwise and use your fingers to remove the seeds. Dice the peeled tomatoes into small cubes. Place the diced tomatoes into a colander and press them gently to remove excess juice.

Combine the tomatoes and the remaining ingredients in a saucepan. Bring to a boil over medium-high heat. Lower the heat and simmer until most of the moisture has dissipated, about 15 to 20 minutes. Remove the pan from the heat and allow the chili sauce to cool to room temperature.

Meanwhile, set up a food mill with a fine or medium disk. Choose a fine disk for a smooth sauce similar to ketchup. Choose a medium disk for a sauce with a slight texture. This is personal preference. Because I generally use chili sauce as a base for cocktail sauce, I like the texture created by the medium disk.

Pour the chili sauce into the food mill and crank the handle to process all the tomatoes. Change direction from time to time to ensure that all the chili sauce is pressed through the disks. You may need to use a rubber scraper to scrape down the sides of the food mill as well.

Pour your finished chili sauce into a sealable glass container and cover. Store in the refrigerator for up to 2 weeks.

WORCESTERSHIRE SAUCE

This Worcestershire sauce is suitable for individuals with gluten sensitivity. Worcestershire sauces often contain malt vinegar derived from barley and soy sauce made with wheat. I've substituted distilled white vinegar and tamari (wheat-free soy sauce) to eliminate the contaminants.

Yield: About 2 cups (475 ml)

Ingredients

½ cup (100 g) sugar

½ cup (120 ml) water

2 cups (475 ml) distilled white vinegar

½ cup (170 g) molasses

1 cup (160 g) diced onion

6 anchovy fillets, chopped

½ cup (120 ml) tamari

2 tablespoons (32 g) tamarind concentrate

4 cloves garlic, crushed

1 small cinnamon stick

1-inch (2.5 cm) piece fresh ginger, slightly crushed

3 tablespoons (33 g) yellow mustard seeds

2 tablespoons (30 g) coarse sea salt or kosher salt

1 teaspoon whole black peppercorns

1 teaspoon whole cloves

5 whole cardamom pods

2-inch (5 cm) piece lime zest, removed with a vegetable peeler

½ teaspoon curry powder

½ teaspoon red pepper flakes

Directions

Combine the sugar and water in a small saucepan. Cook over medium-high heat until it caramelizes, becoming dark amber and syrupy, about 15 minutes. Keep a close eye on the sugar because it can burn quickly, but do not stir.

In the meantime, combine the remaining ingredients in a medium-size saucepan. Bring to a boil over high heat. Lower the heat and simmer for 10 minutes. Add the caramelized sugar and stir well to combine. Simmer the sauce for 5 minutes until the sugar is completely dissolved.

Remove from the heat and allow to cool to room temperature. Pour the sauce into a glass jar with a tight-fitting lid. Refrigerate, covered, for 3 weeks. Strain the sauce to remove the whole spices and return to the sauce to the jar. Refrigerate for up to 8 months. Stir or shake before using.

COCKTAIL SAUCE

I like a little texture to my cocktail sauce, so I use chili sauce
as the base. Ketchup works well, too, if you like a slightly
sweeter flavor and a smoother sauce.

Yield: 1 cup (225 g)

Ingredients

1 cup (275 g) chili sauce *(see page 35)*
    or (240 g) ketchup *(see page 30)*

2 tablespoons (30 g) freshly grated
    or prepared horseradish *(see page 38)*

1 to 2 tablespoons (14 to 28 ml)
    lemon juice

3/4 teaspoon Worcestershire sauce *(see page 36)*

1/2 teaspoon garlic purée *(see page 14)*
    or a pinch of garlic powder

1/2 teaspoon kosher salt or coarse sea salt

1/4 teaspoon ground black pepper

Dash of Tabasco sauce, or more to taste

Directions

Combine all the ingredients in a glass
bowl. Stir to mix well. Cover and refrigerate
for 1 hour before serving so that the flavors
have a chance to meld. Store in the refrigerator, covered, for up to 10 days.

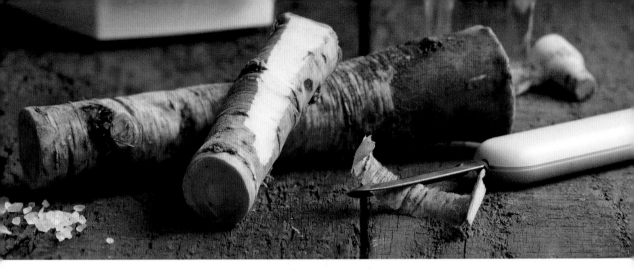

PREPARED HORSERADISH

Horseradish is member of the mustard family, and like its cousins, it can be pretty potent, especially when ground or finely chopped. Make sure that you have good ventilation because the smell can be a little overwhelming. The good news is that it does calm down quickly after being exposed to air.

Yield: 1 cup (240 g)

Ingredients

2 (3- to 4-inch, or 7.5 to 10 cm) pieces of 1 1/4-inch (3 cm) diameter fresh horseradish root

1/4 cup (60 ml) water

2 to 3 tablespoons (28 to 45 ml) distilled white vinegar

1/2 teaspoon coarse sea salt, or to taste

Directions

Peel the horseradish root using a vegetable peeler in the same way you peel a carrot. Trim off the dried ends and cut the peeled root into small cubes. Place the cubes in a blender or food processor. Add the water and vinegar and pulse until finely chopped. For hotter horseradish, wait to add the vinegar until the horseradish is thoroughly pulverized.

Season with salt. Transfer to a sealed container and store in the refrigerator for up to 1 week.

Storing Horseradish

Ideally, fresh horseradish should be store in a sealed container in a cold refrigerator—between 32° and 38°F (0° and 3°C). Prepared horseradish does not have a long shelf life. Once it starts to turn a grayish beige, it's time to toss it.

STEAK SAUCE

This steak sauce follows the classic ingredients but is heartier and far less acidic than the bottled brands. It's delicious on toasted baguette slices with thinly sliced steak, caramelized onions, and blue cheese!

Yield: 1 3/4 cups (420 g)

Ingredients

1/2 cup (75 g) raisins

1 cup (235 ml) boiling water

1 cup (250 g) tomato purée, store-bought or homemade *(see page 40)*

1 cup (235 ml) distilled white vinegar

1/2 small navel orange, peeled, seeded, and coarsely chopped

2 tablespoons (26 g) sugar

2 1/2 teaspoons coarse sea salt or kosher salt, or more to taste

2 teaspoons garlic purée *(see page 17)* or 1/2 teaspoon garlic powder

1 1/2 teaspoons grated onion *(see page 18)* or 1/2 teaspoon onion powder

1/2 teaspoon black pepper

1/4 teaspoon celery seeds

Directions

Place the raisins in a small mixing bowl and cover with the boiling water. Let stand for 30 minutes.

Pour off the water and combine the drained raisins with the remaining ingredients in a blender or food processor. Purée until smooth. Transfer the sauce to a medium-size nonreactive saucepan. Bring to a boil over high heat and then lower the heat and simmer for 30 minutes, stirring occasionally. The mixture should be slightly thickened and syrupy.

Remove the pan from the heat. Allow to cool to room temperature. Season with additional salt, if desired. Pour into a bottle. Cap tightly and refrigerate for up to 3 months.

TOMATO PURÉE

Freshly made tomato purée is so vibrant. Your sauces
will have intense, real tomato flavor.

Yield: About 2 cups (500 g)

Ingredients

2 pounds (910 g) plum tomatoes

1/2 teaspoon salt *(optional)*

Directions

Bring a large pot of water to a boil over
high heat. Meanwhile, notch the base
of each tomato with an X and set aside.
Prepare an ice bath in a large bowl.

When the water starts to boil, add the
tomatoes. Turn off the heat and cover
the pot. Leave the tomatoes in the water
for 5 minutes.

Remove the tomatoes from the hot water
using a slotted spoon and put them into
a bowl of ice water. Let stand for another
5 minutes until the tomatoes are cool
enough to handle.

Drain the tomatoes, core them, and
peel away the skins using your fingers
or a paring knife.

Place a cutting board next to your sink.
Cut the peeled tomatoes in half lengthwise
and scoop the seeds into the sink or a bowl

with your fingers or a teaspoon. (Removing
the seeds will give you a thicker, heartier
purée.) Place the seeded tomatoes into
a colander and press gently to remove
excess juice.

Transfer the tomatoes to a blender or
food processor and purée until smooth.
Your sauce should be pourable, so if
it is too thick, add a little water (not
more juice; tomato juice will increase
the acidity). Process a few seconds longer
to incorporate the added water.

Scrape the puréed tomatoes into a deep
saucepan. Add the salt and stir. Bring
the mixture to a boil over high heat and
then lower the heat and simmer, partly
covered, for 30 minutes. Stir occasionally.
The sauce is done when it has an even,
thick consistency and no liquid separates
from the purée.

If you don't plan to use the purée right
away, transfer it to a sterilized jar *(see page 75).*
Cover and store in the refrigerator for
up to 1 week.

Storing Tomato Purée

If you make larger batches of purée, you can freeze it in small 1- to 2-cup (225 to 455 g) containers. You can also pour the purée into ice cube trays and freeze it. Once the cubes are set, remove them from the trays and store the cubes in freezer bags. You can store it frozen for up to 3 months.

CHAPTER TWO: NUT BUTTERS AND SPREADS

"MAN CANNOT LIVE BY BREAD ALONE; HE MUST HAVE PEANUT BUTTER."

— James A. Garfield, 20th president of the United States

When my younger brother was about five years old, he ate peanut butter and jelly sandwiches almost every day. One day when my mother placed his regular PB&J in front of him, he showed his frustration about something by telling her that unless she complied with his wishes he was going to put his elbow in his sandwich. She told him, "Go ahead. It's your lunch." Glaring at her, he placed his fist under his chin and slowly lowered his elbow into the sandwich. It's my belief that had his sandwich contained some of my homemade peanut butter, he might have reconsidered such drastic actions!

Whether you have children of your own or not, you'll find the recipes contained in this chapter to be delicious and simple. You wouldn't dare put your elbow in your sandwich unless you were a contortionist able to lick your own elbow or had a friend into that sort of thing!

HOMEMADE PEANUT BUTTER

Try your own taste test. Compare your homemade peanut butter to a commercial brand. You won't believe how peanutty the homemade version tastes!

Yield: About 2 cups (520 g)

Ingredients

1 pound (455 g) roasted, shelled Spanish peanuts (about 3 cups [435 g])

1/4 cup (50 g) sugar

3 tablespoons (45 ml) water

1 teaspoon coarse sea salt or kosher salt, or to taste

1/4 cup (60 ml) peanut oil or canola oil *(see Note)*

Directions

Remove the skins from the peanuts by wrapping them, a handful at a time, in a clean kitchen towel and rubbing vigorously. After a minute or two, open the towel and shake the peanuts out over a colander. Work the peanuts with your fingertips to slough off any remaining skins. Continue until all the peanuts are skin free. Set aside.

Combine the sugar and water in a small saucepan. Bring to a boil over high heat, stirring constantly. Cook for 1 to 2 minutes until the mixture thickens slightly. Do not allow the sugar to darken and caramelize. It should be clear and the consistency of light pancake syrup. Remove from the heat.

Place the peanuts and salt in the bowl of a food processor. Grind for 2 to 3 minutes until the peanuts are finely chopped with a gritty, wet-sand appearance. With the motor running, begin to slowly stream the oil into the ground nuts. Continue to process until the peanut butter is smooth and creamy, about 5 to 10 minutes depending on the strength of your food processor. You may need to pause from time to time to scrape down the sides of the bowl.

Next, use a rubber scraper to coax the sugar syrup out of the saucepan into the peanut butter. Process for an additional 1 to 2 minutes to thoroughly incorporate the sugar.

Scrape the contents into a clean jar and refrigerate for up to 6 months.

For chunky peanut butter, place the homemade peanut butter in a mixing bowl. Stir in an additional 1/3 cup (50 g) finely chopped peanuts. When the peanuts are combined, transfer to a clean jar and refrigerate.

Note: Using peanut oil in your peanut butter enhances the flavor.

HONEY PEANUT BUTTER

Honey and peanut butter are natural complements. Don't add too much honey, though, or your peanut butter will seize up!

Yield: About 2 cups (520 g)

Ingredients

1 pound (455 g) shelled, roasted Spanish peanuts (about 3 cups [435 g])

1 teaspoon coarse sea salt or kosher salt, or to taste

1/4 cup (60 ml) peanut oil or canola oil

3 tablespoons (60 g) honey

Directions

Remove the skins from the peanuts by wrapping them, a handful at a time, in a clean kitchen towel and rubbing vigorously. After a minute or two, open the towel and shake the peanuts out over a colander. Work the peanuts with your fingertips to slough off any remaining skins. Continue until all the peanuts are skin free. Set aside.

Place the peanuts and salt in to the bowl of a food processor. Grind the nuts until they form a smooth, thick paste; this can take up to 10 minutes. You may need to scrape down the sides of the bowl from time to time to get an even consistency.

Next, with the motor running, begin to slowly stream in the peanut oil. Continue to process until the peanut butter is smooth and creamy.

In the meantime, gently warm the honey in a saucepan over low heat, or in the microwave, so that it pours more easily. With the food processor running, slowly pour in the warm honey. Process for an additional 1 to 3 minutes until the honey is fully incorporated.

Scrape the contents into a clean jar and refrigerate for up to 6 months.

TIP: Grinding nuts into paste can be pretty taxing on your food processor. You may want to give it a rest for a few minutes in the middle of grinding so that it doesn't overheat.

Peanut or Pea Bean?

Peanuts, or groundnuts, are legumes—meaning they are beans, not nuts. They're a great source of protein dating back to ancient South America. Peruvians made and ate a food similar to peanut butter, but it wasn't until the late 1800s that peanut butter was introduced to the U.S. market. It was originally promoted as a health food, particularly for the elderly.

There are two common misconceptions about peanuts. One is that they belong to the tree nut family like almonds and walnuts. The second is that peanuts grow on the plant roots like potatoes. In fact, peanuts blossom and are pollinated above ground then, once fertilized, the bud dips down to penetrate the soil and the peanuts grow below ground.

Among the types grown in the United States, the four most common are Virginia, Runner, Valencia, and Spanish. Virginia peanuts are sweeter, have the largest kernels, and make up most of the peanuts processed for in-shell eating. The most prolific peanuts are Runners, including Florunners, a variety introduced in the 1970s, which represents more than 80 percent of the peanuts grown in the United States today. Valencias contain three or four small kernels in a long shell and are popularly sold roasted in the shell.

I suggest using Spanish peanuts for a couple of reasons. One, they are a good choice for peanut butter because of their high oil content. Two, they are easy to find. Spanish are small peanuts with reddish brown skin and are processed for peanut candies, peanut oil, and peanut butter.

ALMOND BUTTER

I love a touch of cinnamon in almond butter. Try this spread with apricot jam for a new twist on a PB and J sandwich.

Yield: 1 1/2 cups (390 g)

Ingredients

1/3 cup (75 g) coconut oil

2 cups (220 g) blanched, slivered almonds

1 teaspoon coarse sea salt or kosher salt

3 tablespoons (60 g) honey

1/4 teaspoon ground cinnamon *(optional)*

Directions

Preheat the oven to 350ºF (180ºC, or gas mark 4).

Gently warm the coconut oil in a small saucepan over low heat until it melts. Toss the almonds with 1 tablespoon (14 g) of the melted oil. Spread the nuts on a cookie sheet in a single layer. Bake for 8 to 10 minutes until golden brown, stirring once to ensure even toasting. Keep a close eye on the almonds as they toast to make sure they don't burn. Remove from the oven and let cool to room temperature.

Place the toasted almonds and the salt in a food processor and grind the nuts into a fine paste, about 3 to 5 minutes. Add the honey, the remaining oil, and the cinnamon. Continue processing until the butter becomes smooth. Transfer to a jar and store in the refrigerator for up to 2 months.

Note: Remove the butter from the refrigerator 10 to 15 minutes before use for easier spreading. You can also try adding more coconut oil for a thinner consistency. Experiment with adding 1 tablespoon (14 g) at a time, up to 5 additional (70 g) tablespoons.

I ♥ Coconut Oil

Coconut oil is a wonderful oil to use in nut butter recipes because when blended with nut meal it doesn't separate the way other oils do. That's because coconut oil has a high melting point, about 76º to 78ºF (24º to 25ºC), so it's solid at room temperature. I love using it for almond and cashew butter because both nuts harmonize with the subtle tropical flavor of the oil—think Almond Joy candy bar or Thai coconut curry.

It's also great for high-heat cooking like sautéing or panfrying because it has a relatively high smoke point. That means it doesn't start to smoke and break down until it reaches about 350ºF (180ºC). You can use coconut oil in place of butter or vegetable oils in your recipes, but

remember that it does have a distinctive flavor, so experiment with it when you use it.

Coconut oil also has many health benefits. Although it contains large quantities of saturated fat, coconut oil is actually good for you because it contains about 50 percent lauric acid, a compound that helps prevent various heart problems, including high cholesterol levels and high blood pressure. The saturated fats present in coconut oil have antimicrobial properties as well and can help with various bacteria, fungi, and parasites that cause indigestion. So, it can improve digestion and can soothe various digestive problems, including irritable bowel syndrome. Plus, coconut oil also helps with the absorption of other nutrients, especially vitamins, minerals, and amino acids. Yay, coconut oil!

CASHEW BUTTER

Try a fun tropical fruit sandwich with sliced bananas
or well-drained, crushed pineapple.

Yield: 1 cup (260 g)

Ingredients

1/4 cup (56 g) coconut oil

2 cups (280 g) roasted cashews *(see Note)*

1 tablespoon (15 g) firmly packed
   brown sugar

Pinch of nutmeg *(optional)*

Directions

Preheat the oven to 350ºF (180ºC,
or gas mark 4).

Gently warm the coconut oil in a small
saucepan over low heat until it melts.

Place the cashews and sugar in a food
processor and grind until the nuts are
powdery fine. This can take up to 10 minutes.
Pause occasionally to scrape down the
sides of the bowl.

Next, add the oil and nutmeg and continue
to process until the cashew butter is smooth.
You may need to stop the food processor
from time to time to scrape down the
sides. Transfer the cashew butter to a jar
and refrigerate for up to 2 months.

Note: Most roasted cashews are salted.
If you purchase unsalted cashews, you may
need to add salt. For easy blending, try
adding 1/2 teaspoon sea salt or kosher
salt to the cashews when you first place
them in the food processor.

Cashews—Not as Nutty as You Think!

Although we think of cashews
as nuts, they are, botanically
speaking, seeds. The seeds grow
on the ends of cashew apples, small
pear-shaped fruit. Cashew apples
are edible but quite perishable,
so the fruit is typically only sold
where cashews are grown.

The cashew seed is encased in a
double shell containing a resinous
fluid that is quite toxic, similar to
that of poison ivy. The seeds must
be roasted to remove the resin,
but the smoke released during the
roasting process is so caustic that
roasting is often done outside. After
the roasting process, the shells are
cracked, shelled by hand to remove
the kernels, and then dried, peeled,
and sorted for packaging.

Cashews are high in oil, like
pecans, so they are best stored
in the refrigerator in an airtight
container to maintain freshness.

CHOCOLATE HAZELNUT BUTTER

This creamy chocolate blend can double as an ice cream topping, if you don't have any toast!

To make Chocolate Pecan Butter, substitute 1 1/3 cups (145 g) toasted pecan halves for the hazelnuts.

Yield: About 2 cups (520 g)

Ingredients

1 cup (175 g) semisweet chocolate chips

1/2 cup (120 ml) milk

1/2 cup (60 g) powdered milk

1 rounded tablespoon (20 g) honey

Pinch of sea salt or kosher salt

1/3 cup (48 g) blanched almonds

2/3 cup (90 g) toasted hazelnuts, skins removed *(see Note)*

Directions

Place the chocolate chips in a small mixing bowl and set aside.

In a small saucepan, combine the milk, powdered milk, honey, and salt. Heat over medium heat until the milk just reaches a boil. Remove from the heat and immediately pour over the chocolate chips. Do not stir. Cover the bowl with plastic wrap and let the milk and chocolate rest for 5 minutes.

Meanwhile, place the nuts in a food processor and grind until they are a fine paste. This may take 5 minutes or more of continuous grinding. Stop grinding from time to time to scrape down the sides of the food processor to ensure the nuts are grinding evenly.

Remove the plastic wrap from the mixing bowl and whisk the milk mixture until the chocolate is thoroughly blended. Now, begin to stream the chocolate milk mixture into the food processor. Continue to process until all the milk has been added. Blend until everything is well combined and takes on a glossy finish.

If you'd prefer a smoother texture, pour the entire mixture into a food mill with a medium disk or through a fine-mesh sieve to remove any unground bits of toasted nuts. Transfer to a jar and refrigerate. Use within 1 week.

Note: Toasted hazelnuts are often sold with the skins intact. If the hazelnuts you purchase have the skins on them, simply wrap them in a clean kitchen towel and rub vigorously in the same manner described for Spanish peanuts *(see page 44)*. They don't need to be perfectly clean; just try to slough off as much of the skin as possible.

If you purchase raw hazelnuts, place the nuts on a sheet pan and roast in a 350ºF (180ºC, or gas mark 4) oven for 15 minutes. Let cool and rub off the skins as described above.

MAPLE PECAN BUTTER

The texture of pecan butter is coarser than that of other nut butters due to the golden brown outer layer of the kernel. Although it lacks smooth creaminess, the flavor is outstanding. Try it on quick breads like banana, zucchini, or pumpkin.

Yield: About 1 cup (260 g)

Ingredients

6 1/2 ounces (182 g) pecan pieces

Coarse sea salt or kosher salt, to taste

1 tablespoon (15 ml) canola oil

2 tablespoons (40 g) maple syrup

1/4 teaspoon vanilla extract

Pinch of cinnamon *(optional)*

Directions

Preheat a large skillet over medium heat for 5 minutes. Pour in the pecans and toast, stirring often, until fragrant, 3 to 5 minutes.

Pour the toasted pecans into a food processor, add a pinch of salt, and blend until creamy and smooth, about 5 minutes. Pause from time to time to scrape down the sides of the food processor with a spatula. Add the oil and process until blended. Next add the maple syrup, vanilla, and cinnamon and blend again to combine, about 5 minutes. The maple syrup will cause a thickening in the nut butter. Continue to process until the butter releases and becomes creamy again.

Pour into a clean glass jar, cover, and refrigerate for up to 2 months. If the oil separates from the nut butter, simply bring to room temperature and stir to combine.

TIP: Pecan Pointers

This American native is a cousin of the hickory nut. Pecans contain more than 70 percent fat, so shelled nuts should be stored in airtight containers in the refrigerator to preserve freshness. Although pecans are available year-round, peak season occurs in the fall—just in time for pecan pie!

TAHINI (SESAME SEED PASTE)

Tahini is the base for some of my favorite dips and dressings—Hummus *(see page 158)*, Baba Ghanoush *(see page 160)*, and Sesame Tahini Dressing *(see page 98)*.

Yield: ½ *cup (120 g)*

Ingredients

¾ cup (109 g) hulled white sesame seeds

¼ teaspoon coarse sea salt or kosher salt, or more to taste

2 tablespoons (28 ml) toasted sesame oil

1 tablespoon (15 ml) olive oil

Directions

Warm a medium-size sauté pan over medium heat for 3 to 5 minutes. Add the sesame seeds. Toast the seeds, tossing or stirring regularly, for 10 to 15 minutes, until they begin to turn golden brown. Be careful not to let them burn.

Remove the pan from the heat and pour the toasted sesame seeds onto a large sheet of parchment paper or waxed paper to cool.

Form the parchment paper into a funnel and pour the cooled seeds and a pinch of salt into a spice mill, coffee grinder, or mini food processor. Pulse until they are ground into a fine paste. When the seeds have formed a paste, add the sesame oil and olive oil. Keep pulsing until the paste is smooth and creamy. Scrape the paste into a sealable container and refrigerate for up to 1 month.

Note: Due to the high oil content in sesame seeds, they are prone to rancidity and should be stored in the refrigerator to maintain freshness.

REDFIELD FARM APPLE BUTTER

I was inspired to write this recipe in honor of Ann Redfield, the Quaker heroine of *Redfield Farm: A Novel of the Underground Railroad*, by Judith Redline Coopey (my mom). The apple butter is as delightful as the book. Try it on a grilled cheese sandwich with sharp Cheddar, alongside a pork roast, or smeared on toast.

Yield: Two 1-pint (475 ml) jars

Ingredients

2 pounds (910 g) Granny Smith apples, washed, quartered, and cored

1 cup (235 ml) water

1/2 cup (100 g) sugar

3-inch (7.5 cm) cinnamon stick

4 whole cloves

4 whole allspice

Directions

In a large saucepan, combine the apples and water. Bring to a boil over high heat and then lower the heat and simmer until the apples have softened to the consistency of applesauce, 20 to 25 minutes.

Pass the apples through a sieve or food mill. Stir in the sugar and spices and pour the apple purée into a slow cooker. Set the temperature on low. Cover and cook, stirring occasionally, for 6 to 8 hours. Use a slotted spoon to remove the whole spices.

At this point you can "put up" the hot apple butter in sterilized canning jars *(see page 75)* or simply cool the mixture and store it in the refrigerator for up to 3 weeks.

Apples to Apples

I suggest using Granny Smith apples for apple butter, but does it really matter which type of apple you use? Well, yes, but there's more to it. Here's a little primer for some of the more common apple varieties:

Golden Delicious—These are a nice all-purpose apple, with a mild, sweet, distinctive flavor. Be careful not to store them too long because they shrivel and can bruise easily. They are very nice for pies and salads.

Granny Smith—These have a gorgeous bright green skin with a rosy blush when very ripe. Firm, crisp, and tart, these apples are best paired with salty cheeses and savory foods when eaten raw. They sweeten when cooked and make wonderful pie apples. Granny Smith are my favorite choice for caramel apples because their tartness balances the sweetness of the caramel.

Jonagold—A hybrid of Golden Delicious and Jonathan apples, Jonagolds are a nice balance of sweet and tart. Firm and juicy, they will keep in the refrigerator for up to 3 months. They can be used in almost any apple recipe.

Gala—These are similar in shape to the Red Delicious but feature a mottled red and bright yellow skin. They are firm, juicy, and fine-textured with yellowish white flesh. Their sweet, slightly tart flavor makes them good for both cooking and eating raw.

Fuji—Developed in Japan and introduced to the United States in the 1980s, Fuji apples are intensely sweet and slightly acidic, with a crisp juicy flesh. They are great eaten raw alone or in salads, but lose consistency when cooked.

McIntosh—Very juicy with soft skin and crisp flesh, they can become mealy if stored too long. They are nice for eating or making applesauce, but they will get mushy when baked.

Red Delicious—This is the ubiquitous apple of the media, think Snow White and the Wicked Witch. Characterized by their deep red color, Red Delicious are a reliable, crisp apples, perfect for eating raw.

PUMPKIN PURÉE

You can use this purée for pumpkin butter *(see page 58)* or in your favorite pumpkin pie or pumpkin bread recipe.

Yield: 2 to 3 cups (490 to 735 g)

Ingredients
1 (6- to 8-inch, or 15 to 20 cm) "pie" pumpkin (Sugar Pie, Cinderella, Lumina, etc.) *(see sidebar)*

Directions
Wash the pumpkin exterior using warm water or a commercial vegetable wash. Pat the pumpkin dry and pop off the stem, if it's still attached. Slice the pumpkin in half, lengthwise from the stem to the butt of the pumpkin.

Lay the pumpkin open on a flat surface and use a large spoon to remove the seeds and pulp. You can cook the pumpkin in a number of ways—steaming, microwaving, or roasting. I prefer roasting because it enhances the natural sweetness, but I include all three methods here.

Steaming—Cut the pumpkin into quarters or eighths. Select a large pot with a lid. Place a steamer insert/basket in the bottom of the pot. Add water to come up to the base of the steamer. Place the filled pot on the stove top over high heat. When the water begins to steam, add the pumpkin and cover. Steam until the pumpkin is soft, about 20 to 30 minutes depending on the size of the pumpkin. The flesh should be easy to scoop away with a spoon when it is done. Set aside to cool.

Microwaving—Cut the pumpkin into eighths or smaller chunks. Place the chunks in a microwave-safe bowl. Pour 1 to 2 inches (2.5 to 5 cm) of water into the bowl. Microwave on high for 15 minutes. Check to see if the pumpkin is soft by puncturing it with a fork. If the pumpkin is not completely soft, continue to microwave on high in 3 to 5-minute intervals until it's done. Depending on the size of the chunks, it can take 15 to 30 minutes to cook completely. The flesh should be easy to scoop away with a spoon when it is done. Set aside to cool.

Roasting—Preheat the oven to 350ºF (180ºC, or gas mark 4). Place the halved pumpkin cut-side down on a rimmed baking sheet or large casserole. Pour boiling water around the pumpkin, about 1/2 inch (1.3 cm) deep. Carefully cover the pumpkin with aluminum foil. Place the baking sheet or casserole pan in the oven. Cook for about 45 minutes to 1 hour until the pumpkin is very soft. The flesh should be easy to scoop away with a spoon when it is done. Set aside to cool.

When the pumpkin is cool enough to handle, use a large spoon (a tablespoon

"Pie" Pumpkins

Although all pumpkins are edible, some are better suited for puréeing. I suggest choosing a "pie" variety because they are generally sweeter and have a texture that's less grainy than jack-o'-lantern types. Many grocery stores carry pie pumpkins in late September through December. There are many varieties available depending on where you live, including the Sugar Pie, New England Pie, Lumina, and Cinderella. Most pie pumpkins are only about 8 inches (20 cm) in diameter. When selecting a pie pumpkin, choose one that is firm, without bruises or soft spots, and a good orange color—or in the case of a Lumina, a ghostly white color.

or serving spoon) to scoop the cooked pumpkin from the skin. It should scoop away easily.

Place the pumpkin flesh into a blender and purée until smooth. Alternatively, process the pumpkin flesh through a food mill using a medium or fine disk. The purée should be thick like canned pumpkin purée. If your pumpkin purée is watery, place it in a clean towel, pull the ends up into a knot, and suspend over a bowl overnight.

The pumpkin is now ready to be used in your favorite recipe—pumpkin butter, pumpkin pie, or pumpkin bread. It can also be stored in the refrigerator for up to 1 week or placed in airtight containers and frozen for up to 3 months.

PUMPKIN BUTTER

If you like apple butter, you should give pumpkin butter a try.
It's like pumpkin pie for your toast!

Yield: About 2 cups (490 g)

Ingredients

2 cups (490 g) pumpkin purée,
   preferably homemade *(see page 56)*

1/2 cup (115 g) firmly packed brown sugar

1 teaspoon ground cinnamon

1/4 teaspoon nutmeg

Pinch of ground cloves

Apple cider, if needed *(optional)*

Directions

Mix all the ingredients together in a
medium-size saucepan. Bring to a boil
over high heat and then decrease the
heat to medium-low. Simmer slowly
for 1 hour, stirring occasionally.

If you feel that the pumpkin butter is not
thick enough, simply continue to cook it
until it reaches the thickness you prefer.

If you feel that the pumpkin butter is
too thick, you can add a little apple cider
to thin it. Add it slowly, just 1 tablespoon
(15 ml) at a time, until you achieve the
desired thickness.

For a creamy, smoother consistency,
you can whip the pumpkin butter in a
blender. Allow the butter to cool slightly
before blending to avoid splattering the
hot liquid. Transfer the finished butter
to a sterilized jar *(see page 75)*. Cover and
refrigerate for up to 3 weeks.

PLUM BUTTER WITH CHINESE FIVE-SPICE POWDER

This plum butter has a sweet-tart taste that makes it pop with flavor. It's a favorite on raisin toast in our house. You can also warm it up to use as a sauce or glaze for roast pork, turkey, or duck.

Yield: About 1 1/2 cups (370 g)

Ingredients

2 pounds (910 g) plums

1 cup (235 ml) water

1 cup (200 g) sugar

1 teaspoon Chinese five-spice powder

Pinch of coarse sea salt or kosher salt

Directions

Fill a large pot with water and bring to a boil over high heat.

Fill a large mixing bowl with half ice and half water to make an ice bath. Place the bowl in the sink.

When the water is boiling, gently add the plums and blanch the plums for 1 to 2 minutes. The thin skin will start to crack quickly. Remove the plums from the boiling water with a slotted spoon and plunge them into the ice bath.

When the plums have cooled enough to handle, peel away the skins with your fingers or a paring knife. Cut the plums in halves or quarters to remove the pits.

Place the peeled, pitted plums in a medium saucepan. Add the water. Bring to a boil over high heat and then decrease the heat slightly so that the plums maintain a low boil. Cook until the texture of the plums is soft and smooth, about 15 minutes.

Stir in the sugar, Chinese five-spice powder, and salt. Continue cooking, stirring occasionally, until the plums have reduced to a jam-like spreadable consistency. This should take about 1 to 1 1/2 hours. When the plum butter has thickened to your liking, remove it from the heat and pour into a sterilized jar *(see page 75)*. Cover and refrigerate for up to 4 weeks.

Chinese Five-Spice Powder

If you've never tried Chinese five-spice powder, you are in for a treat. It's an intoxicating blend of fennel seed, cinnamon, ginger, star anise, and cloves common to many Chinese dishes, stir-fries, marinades, and sauces. I think it's to die for on pork tenderloins and pan-seared duck breasts, and if you enjoy drinking Pinot Noir, you've found your new favorite spice blend.

VANILLA CHAI PEAR BUTTER

This soft, fragrant fruit butter is scrumptious
on a warm croissant.

Yield: About 2 cups (490 g)

Ingredients

1 ½ pounds (680 g) ripe pears,
   peeled, cored, and diced

1 ½ cups (355 ml) water

2 chai tea bags or 2 teaspoons loose-leaf
   chai tea wrapped in a square of
   cheesecloth and tied with some
   kitchen string (I use Tazo brand tea)

½ cup (100 g) sugar

½ teaspoon vanilla extract

1 tablespoon (15 ml) freshly squeezed
   lemon juice

Pinch of coarse sea salt or kosher salt

Directions

Place the pears, water, and chai tea bags
in a medium-size saucepan. Bring to a boil
over high heat. Lower the heat and simmer
until the pears are soft and mushy, about
30 minutes. Remove from the heat and
allow to cool to room temperature.

When the pears have cooled, remove
the tea bags. Purée the cooled fruit
in a food processor or blender until
smooth. Return the puréed pears to the
saucepan. Stir in the sugar and vanilla.
Bring the purée to a low boil and cook,
stirring regularly, until the purée has
thickened and is spreadable, about 1 to 1 ½
hours. The butter will thicken slightly
as it cools; however, make sure you feel
it is thick enough before you remove it
from the heat—think jam. Don't be afraid
to cook it longer to get the thickness
you prefer.

When the butter has thickened, remove it
from the heat and stir in the lemon juice
and a pinch of salt. Pour the butter into a
clean jar and refrigerate for up to 2 weeks.

Fruit Butter vs. Jam

Frankly, I'm just too lazy to make
jam! I love to make fruit butters
because of how quickly and easily
you can make them. Plus, they are
far less complicated. You don't
need to worry about pectin ratios
or whether your spread will be too
runny; you simply simmer the
fruit until it reaches spreadable
consistency. Done!

TRIPLE CITRUS CURD

This curd makes a delightful parfait when layered with fresh tropical fruit or berries and whipped cream. I also love it on New York cheesecake!

Yield: About 1 1/2 cups (480 g)

Ingredients

Zest *(see note)* and juice from 2 limes
(about 1/4 cup [60 ml] juice)

Zest and juice from 1 lemon (about
2 tablespoons [28 ml] juice)

Zest and juice from 1 orange
(about 1/4 cup [60 ml] juice)

1 cup (200 g) sugar

4 egg yolks, lightly beaten

Pinch of coarse sea salt or
kosher salt, to taste

6 tablespoons (84 g) cold unsalted
butter, cut into small cubes

Directions

Using a vegetable peeler, remove the zest from the citrus *(see Note)*. Try not to include too much of the white pith. Keep the lime zest separate. Mince the lime zest finely and set aside.

Place the peeled lemon and orange zest in the top of a double boiler or in a medium-size stainless steel mixing bowl. Juice all the fruit. Pour the juice into the double boiler/mixing bowl along with the sugar, egg yolks, and salt. Whisk to combine.

Add about 1 inch (2.5 cm) water to the base of the double boiler or medium-size saucepan. Bring the water to a simmer.

Place the double-boiler pan or stainless steel mixing bowl over the simmering water and decrease the heat to low. Whisk the juice mixture constantly until it begins to thicken, about 20 to 25 minutes. The curd will thicken just below a simmer at about 170ºF (77ºC). Remove the thickened curd from the heat and add the chilled butter. Whisk vigorously until the mixture is glossy and smooth.

Pour the curd through a sieve into a small bowl. Mix in the reserved lime zest. Cover with a piece of plastic wrap, pressing the wrap snuggly against the curd. Refrigerate for up to 2 weeks.

Note: I like to use a Microplane zester/grater for the lime zest. It makes a light, fluffy zest that's perfect for finishing the curd.

> **TIP:** Fruit curds make wonderful cake fillings. Also try them spread on pancakes, waffles, and French toast.

LEMON CURD

Lemon curd on blueberry scones is like heaven.
Or, fill a baked tart shell with lemon curd and top with
a few raspberries for a delightful dessert.

Yield: 1 1/2 cups (480 g)

Ingredients

Zest and juice from 6 lemons
  (at least 1/2 cup [120 ml] juice)

1 cup (200 g) sugar

1 whole egg

4 egg yolks

Pinch of coarse sea salt or
  kosher salt, to taste

1/2 cup (112 g) cold unsalted butter,
  cut into small cubes

Directions

Using a vegetable peeler, remove the zest from the citrus. Try not to include too much of the white pith or the curd will be bitter. Mince the zest finely.

Place the lemon zest in the top of a double boiler or in a medium-size stainless steel mixing bowl. Pour the juice into the double boiler/mixing bowl along with the sugar, egg, egg yolks, and salt. Whisk to combine.

Add about 1 inch (2.5 cm) water to the base of the double boiler or medium-size saucepan. Bring the water to a simmer. Place the double-boiler pan or stainless steel mixing bowl over the simmering water and decrease the heat to low. Whisk the juice mixture constantly until it begins to thicken, about 20 to 25 minutes. The curd will thicken just below a simmer at about 170ºF (77ºC). Remove the thickened curd from the heat and add the chilled butter. Whisk vigorously until the mixture is glossy and smooth.

Pour the curd through a sieve into a small bowl. Cover with a piece of plastic wrap, pressing the wrap snuggly against the curd. Refrigerate for up to 2 weeks.

Variation: **Lemon Thyme Curd**—Add two 4-inch (10 cm) sprigs fresh thyme to the lemon juice, sugar, and eggs while warming the mixture in a double boiler. Remove the sprigs when sieving the thickened curd.

It's Just a Curd to Me!

I got to wondering about the origin of fruit curd. As a Wisconsin native prior to the age of eighteen, I would have defined it as a squeaky (orally and aurally) chunk of fresh cheese. Later, I experienced the sublime pleasure of a freshly baked scone with clotted cream and lemon curd. Life changer.

Like so many culinary terms, curd doesn't seem to be an obvious name for the creamy sweet-tart substance of scone fame. I've researched the origin story and come up blank. Lemon curd, also called lemon cheese, shows up in cookbooks in nineteenth-century Britain. It has been a staple ever since. If I were going to speculate, I would guess that perhaps people related the thickened spread to potted cheese or soft, spreadable curds. It's just one of life's delicious mysteries.

ORANGE FLOWER CURD

You don't have to use the orange flower water in this recipe, but it adds a delicate floral flavor you just can't duplicate. Try this orange curd over vanilla ice cream for a grown-up Dreamsicle experience!

Yield: About 1 1/4 cups (300 g)

Ingredients

Zest and juice from 2 oranges
   (1/2 cup [120 ml] juice*)

2 tablespoons (28 ml) freshly
   squeezed lemon juice

2/3 cup (132 g) sugar

4 egg yolks, lightly beaten

Pinch of sea salt or kosher salt

6 tablespoons (84 g) cold unsalted
   butter, cut into small cubes

1/2 teaspoon orange flower water *(optional)*

Directions

Using a vegetable peeler, remove the zest from the oranges. Try not to include too much of the white pith. Slice the zest into thin strips. Place the strips of zest in the top of a double boiler or in a medium-size stainless steel mixing bowl. Add the orange juice, lemon juice, sugar, egg yolks, and salt. Whisk to combine.

Add 1 inch (2.5 cm) water to the base of the double boiler or medium-size saucepan. Bring the water to a boil. Place the double-boiler pan or stainless steel mixing bowl over the boiling water and decrease the heat to medium-low to maintain a simmer. Whisk the juice mixture constantly until it begins to thicken, about 20 to 25 minutes. The curd will thicken just below a simmer at about 170ºF (77ºC). Remove the thickened curd from the heat and add the chilled butter. Whisk vigorously until the mixture is glossy and smooth. Add the orange flower water and whisk to combine.

Pour the curd through a sieve into a small bowl or glass jar to remove the zest. Cover with a piece of plastic wrap or a snug-fitting lid. Chill for at least 1 hour prior to using. Refrigerate for up to 2 weeks.

* Add store-bought orange juice to equal 1/2 cup (120 ml), if necessary.

***Variations:* Orange Rosemary Curd**—Omit the orange flower water. Add one 4-inch (10 cm) sprig of fresh rosemary to the juice, sugar, and eggs before warming.

Orange Cardamom Curd—Omit the orange flower water. Whisk in 1/4 teaspoon ground cardamom to the juice, sugar, and eggs before warming.

Orange Flower Water

Imagine standing in an orange grove at dusk, and a warm breeze fills your nose with delicate perfume. The sweetness tickles your nose; you can almost taste it—exotic, yet familiar. That's orange flower water.

I started using orange flower water, also called orange blossom water, several years ago when I began experimenting with Moroccan food. I think it's one of the most unique ingredients I've ever worked with.

It's really just what it sounds like; blossoms from fragrant orange trees are steamed and distilled to a delicate concentration/infusion. It's used in a variety of recipes

from French pastries to Mediterranean baklavas to Middle Eastern savory rice dishes and drinks and even cocktails. Orange flower water is a quintessential Moroccan ingredient that I use when teaching students to infuse a subtle but heady, blossom sweetness to carrot salads and coconut cakes.

I think it takes the orange curd to a whole new level. When you first taste the curd, you get a subtle whiff of blossoms and then the silky citrus fills your mouth. It adds an intense, somewhat intangible oomph.

You can find orange flower water in Middle Eastern markets, specialty stores, or online at Chefshop.com *(see Resources)*.

CHAPTER THREE: SALAD DRESSINGS

"IT TAKES FOUR MEN TO DRESS A SALAD: A WISE MAN FOR THE SALT, A MADMAN FOR THE PEPPER, A MISER FOR THE VINEGAR, AND A SPENDTHRIFT FOR THE OIL."

— *Spanish proverb*

I've been making my own salad dressings for years. At first I dabbled with creating vinaigrettes, choosing interesting combinations of vinegars and oils. Later, I began experimenting with creamy styles; it was more about being adventurous than anything else. I wanted to see if I could come up with my own versions of typical bottled dressings, but a funny thing happened along the way. I discovered that I couldn't go back to the commercial brands. They simply didn't taste as good as I once thought. They tasted too sugary, or too acidic, or oddly synthetic. I can't wait for you to try your hand at some of these recipes. You, my friend, may find yourself in the same delicious dilemma!

HOMEMADE WINE VINEGAR

The yield for the homemade wine vinegar varies according to the container you choose (evaporation), how much wine you add, and the length of time you ferment, but you should end up with at least 1 quart (950 ml).

Yield: About 1 quart (950 ml)

Equipment

Crock or gallon-size (4 L) iced-tea jar *(see Note)*

Cheesecloth or linen napkin

Kitchen string or rubber band

Sterilized bottles with corks or screw tops

Ingredients

2 cups (475 ml) good-quality fruity
   red wine like zinfandel or merlot,
   plus extra for feeding

1 cup (235 ml) water

8 ounces (225 g) vinegar starter *(see page 71)*

1 bay leaf *(optional)*

Directions

Wash the crock with hot soapy water. Rinse thoroughly and drain. Pour the wine and water into the clean crock. Next add the vinegar starter.

Cover the wine crock with cheesecloth and secure it with string or a rubber band. Place the bay leaf on top of the cheesecloth. The bay leaf will help keep fruit flies away. You may want to replace the leaf every few weeks, as it dries.

Place the covered crock in a warm, dark place, like a cupboard or pantry. If the vinegar is too cold, the bacteria growth will be slow. Ideally, the temperature should be around 75°F (24°C), but anything between 60° and 85°F (15° and 29°C) should work.

Check the mixture in a week and a half; you should begin to see a shiny layer forming on top of the wine. Over time, the layer will thicken. This is normal. It's the mother growing, turning the wine alcohol into vinegar.

Now it's time to begin feeding the vinegar with more wine. It's important to try not to disturb the mother too much, so I suggest using a plastic turkey baster with the bulb removed as a long funnel. (You can also place a funnel on top of the turkey baster to make it easier to fill.) Simply slide the baster tip underneath an edge of the mother at the side of the crock. Pour about 2 1/2 cups (570 ml) wine into the crock through the baster/funnel. Wait about 5 days and repeat the feeding process. Then wait another 5 days and feed again.

Now, it's just about waiting—about 2 to 3 months. During this time, try not to disturb the mother but do continue to feed the vinegar 1/2 to 1 cup (120 to 235 ml) wine every week or so. I wish I could give you a specific date that would guarantee that your vinegar would be done, but making homemade vinegar isn't an exact science, so you'll have to use your nose. After 2 to 3 months, give it a whiff. Does it have a vinegar smell, as opposed to a sweeter wine smell? Good. Next, gently move the mother aside and look at the vinegar. Is it a slightly lighter color than the wine you started with? Another good sign! Now taste. I suggest using a plastic spoon to taste because metal spoons can give the vinegar a weird flavor. If it tastes like vinegar, it's ready to use.

The mother should be transferred to a new mixture, or discarded, once the vinegar is ready to use. Remove the mother, either by gently lifting it out with a large spoon or ladle or by pouring it through a sieve. You will probably have several layers of mothers—kind of like gelatinous, semi-translucent pancakes. Save the softest ones for your next batch of vinegar. They are the youngest and hungriest.

The vinegar itself should be poured through a coffee filter–lined funnel into sterilized bottles (*see page 75*) for storage. The vinegar will mellow over time, but if you feel the flavor is too pungent, you can cut the vinegar with a little water to reduce the strength.

Note: In general, a crock seems to work best for making vinegar. The idea is that you want to expose as much of the wine as possible to air, but not expose it to too much light. The larger opening of a crock works better than, say, a mason jar. Plus, exposing the vinegar to light slows down the transformation process, so if you use an iced-tea jar, you should store it in a cupboard or place it in a cardboard box.

A Little Mothering Advice

Although the bacteria that create the fermentation process occur naturally in the environment, using a vinegar starter can speed the process. Vinegar starters, also called vinegar mothers, are available in many home-brewing stores, wine-making supply stores, and online.

Another option is to use a mother from a naturally fermented vinegar in your cupboard. Traditionally, wine vinegar is made through a slow fermentation process—in barrels or vats over a period of months. However, many commercially prepared vinegars speed the process by oxygenating the mixture, filtering out

much of the bacteria and sediment, and then pasteurizing the vinegar to stop the bacterial growth. However, if you notice a cloudy, jellyfish-looking mass in the bottom of one of your vinegar bottles, you're in luck—that's the mother! Simply pour the mother into your wine crock.

Why Red Wine?

For some reason white wine vinegar takes longer to make than does red wine vinegar. After you've successfully made red wine vinegar, you can use your mother to start some white wine vinegar. It may take as long as 6 months to transform.

Garlic Dill Vinegar

This vinegar is phenomenal in potato salad.

Yield: 2 cups (475 ml)

Ingredients

6 to 8 sprigs fresh dill or 1 tablespoon (4 g)
   dried dillweed

2 cloves garlic

4 peppercorns

2 cups (475 ml) cider vinegar

Directions

Wash the dill sprigs. Pat dry and crush the herbs gently with your fingers. Put the crushed herbs into a sterilized pint (475 ml) jar *(see page 75)*. Add the garlic and peppercorns. Fill the jar with the vinegar.

Close the lid and place the jar in a cool, dark place, like a pantry cupboard, for at least 1 week, gently shaking the jar every day or so to mix the flavors of the herbs.

Strain the flavored vinegar through a funnel lined with cheesecloth to remove the herbs and spices. Pour the strained vinegar into a sterilized bottle. If you'd like, you can add a few fresh sprigs of dill, or a few dill seed heads, into the bottle for decoration. Store the strained vinegar for up to 6 months.

Chive-Blossom Vinegar

If you grow chives, snip a few blossoms for this flavorful vinegar.

Yield: 4 cups (950 ml)

Ingredients

1 cup (48 g) freshly snipped chive blossoms

4 cups (950 ml) white wine vinegar

Directions

Gently rinse the chive blossoms in a bowl of cool water. Drain and pat dry with a clean kitchen towel.

Place the clean blossoms in a sterilized, quart-size (950 ml) glass jar *(see page 75)*. Pour the vinegar over the blossoms. Seal the jar tightly and store in a dark place for 2 weeks. Shake the jar from time to time.

Little by little, the blossoms will begin to lose their color, and the vinegar will turn pale pink. At the end of the 2 weeks, strain the vinegar through a cheesecloth-lined funnel into a sterilized bottle. Cork tightly. Store for up to 6 months.

TARRAGON VINEGAR

Tarragon vinegar is a classic.

Yield: 2 cups (475 ml)

Ingredients

8 to 10 sprigs fresh tarragon *(see Note)*

2 cups (475 ml) white or red wine vinegar *(see page 70)*

Directions

Gently rinse the fresh tarragon and pat dry with a clean kitchen towel.

Bruise the stems and leaves of the tarragon by rubbing them between your fingertips. Bruising the herb will help release the flavor into the vinegar. Place the tarragon in a sterilized wide-mouth glass jar *(see page 75)*.

Fill the jar with the wine vinegar. Seal the jar with a tight-fitting lid. Place it in a cool, dark place. Allow the vinegar to rest for 6 weeks. Shake it occasionally to help blend the flavors.

Line a funnel with cheesecloth and strain the vinegar through it into a sterilized bottle. If you'd like, add a fresh sprig of tarragon to the bottle for decoration.

Note: If you purchase your fresh tarragon from a grocery store, you may want to wash it with a vegetable wash or mild detergent to remove possible pesticides. Be sure to rinse it thoroughly to wash away any detergent residue prior to using it for vinegar.

If you grow your own tarragon, try to pick it before it flowers. The strength of the herb diminishes as it cycles into flower.

GARLIC VINEGAR

Add a little oomph to your Caesar salad dressing
or vinaigrette with this delicious piquant vinegar.
Be sure to use fresh garlic for the best flavor.

Yield: 2 cups (475 ml)

Ingredients

6 cloves garlic

2 cups (475 ml) white wine vinegar

Directions

Peel the garlic using a garlic peeler or by hand. Take care to be gentle so the garlic doesn't bruise and split. Damaged garlic can sometimes cause the vinegar to discolor.

Place the garlic in a sterilized pint jar or wide-mouth bottle *(see tip)*. Pour in the vinegar. Cover with a tight-fitting lid. Place in a cool, dark place (pantry or cupboard) for 2 weeks. Shake the container from time to time.

At the end of the 2 weeks, strain the vinegar to remove the garlic, if desired. Store the infused vinegar in a sterilized bottle or jar for up to 6 months.

> **TIP: How to Sterilize Bottles and Jars**
> Many recipes in this book suggest storing finished recipes in sterilized jars and bottles. Sterilizing helps ensure less bacterial growth and longer, safer storage. To sterilize, fill each jar or bottle with hot water and place it in a deep pot. Fill the pot with water enough to cover the jars by at least 1 inch (2.5 cm). Bring the pot to a boil and boil for 10 minutes. Carefully remove the jars or bottles from the liquid using tongs or a jar lifter. Pour out the hot water and then either immediately fill with whatever you are pickling or bottling or allow to air-dry.

STANDARD VINAIGRETTE

Fresh quality ingredients make all the difference. Once you get in the habit of making your own salad dressings, you'll find bottled dressings to be overly sweetened, salty messes.

Yield: 1 cup (235 ml)

Ingredients

1/4 cup (60 ml) red wine vinegar *(see page 70)* or white wine vinegar

2 tablespoons (20 g) minced shallot

1 tablespoon (4 g) minced fresh herbs, singularly or combination: parsley, chives, tarragon, chervil, or marjoram

Pinch of dried thyme

3/4 cup (175 ml) extra-virgin olive oil

1/2 teaspoon kosher salt or sea salt, or to taste

1/4 teaspoon freshly ground black pepper, or to taste

Directions

Combine the vinegar, shallot, fresh herbs, and dried thyme in a medium-size mixing bowl. Whisk to blend. Then slowly add the olive oil, whisking constantly. Season with salt and pepper and serve.

Note: This dressing will begin to separate immediately after mixing. Not to worry: simply give it a stir just before using or toss with the entire salad just before serving.

Variations: The standard vinaigrette is the base for a whole host of variations. Here are a few for you to try:

Blue Cheese Vinaigrette—This is great on a hearty green salad or sliced tomatoes with sweet onions. Choose red wine vinegar and 1/3 cup (40 g) blue cheese crumbles.

Olive and Caper Vinaigrette—The tangy goodness is perfect for a grilled tuna or salmon salad. Omit tarragon from the fresh herbs and add 2 teaspoons minced green olives and 2 teaspoons minced, rinsed capers.

Anchovy Herb Vinaigrette—If you like Caesar salad, you should give this a try. Select parsley as your fresh herb and add 1 teaspoon anchovy paste or mashed anchovies and 1 teaspoon minced, rinsed capers. For a little kick, try a dash of Tabasco sauce, too.

Tomato Curry Vinaigrette—This is lovely over delicate baby greens. Omit the fresh herbs and add 1/4 cup (70 g) chili sauce *(see page 35)* and 1/4 teaspoon sweet curry powder.

Mustard Vinaigrette—This is a wonderful standard. The mustard helps the vinaigrette stay blended. Add 2 tablespoons (22 g) Dijon mustard *(see page 29)* and 1 teaspoon Worcestershire sauce *(see page 36)*.

Horseradish Vinaigrette—This is perfect for a flat-iron or flank steak salad. Use parsley and/or chives for the fresh herbs and add 1 1/2 tablespoons (23 g) prepared horseradish *(see page 38)*.

BALSAMIC VINAIGRETTE

On its own, balsamic vinegar can lack the acidic pop to make a good vinaigrette. I usually add a little red wine vinegar to help balance the dressing. This dressing is incredibly versatile. Try using it as a marinade for chicken.

Yield: 1 1/4 cups (295 ml)

Ingredients

1/4 cup (60 ml) balsamic vinegar

2 tablespoons (28 ml) red wine vinegar *(see page 70)*

1 teaspoon Dijon mustard *(see page 28 or 29)*

1 teaspoon dried basil or 2 teaspoons minced fresh basil

1 teaspoon dried parsley flakes or 2 teaspoons minced fresh parsley *(see page 14)*

1/2 teaspoon sugar

3/4 cup (175 ml) extra-virgin olive oil

1/2 teaspoon sea salt or kosher salt, or to taste

Freshly ground pepper, to taste

Directions

In a small mixing bowl, combine the balsamic vinegar, red wine vinegar, mustard, basil, parsley, and sugar. Whisk to combine. Slowly add the olive oil, whisking constantly to thoroughly blend. Season with salt and pepper and serve. Or better yet, if you have time to let it rest before serving, the flavors will intensify. I like to give my vinaigrette about an hour to rest to fuse the flavors.

If you have any unused dressing, cover it and store it in the refrigerator for up to 3 days. After that, the flavor begins to wane.

Note: The mustard creates an emulsion, meaning the liquid stays blended instead of separating immediately, but you may need to stir the dressing again just before serving.

Extra-Virgin Olive Oil—You Don't Always Get What You Pay For

I think most of us believe that "extra-virgin" means quality. In fact, the dictionary defines "extra-virgin" as the highest quality olive oil derived from the first pressing of olives. But here's the problem: although there are international standards, fraud is rampant in the olive oil industry. Fraudulent manu-factures pass off low-quality, chemically treated olive oil blends as extra-virgin every day. As recently as 2012, Spanish police discovered a large-scale operation blending palm, avocado, and sunflower oils with olive oil. Incidentally, Spain happens to be the largest exporter of olive oil in the world.

So why should we care? Well, if you're buying olive oil for the health benefit (lowering your risk of heart disease, lowering cholesterol, etc.), you may not be getting what you pay for. Blended oils just aren't as good. In addition, there could be health concerns for people with food allergies and sensitivities.

Although the USDA defines standard grades of olive oil, including "virgin" and "extra-virgin," it's not an enforcement agency. The standards are voluntary and only apply to U.S. olive oils. So, if you see "extra-virgin" on a $10 bottle of imported olive oil, you should probably just consider it a marketing term rather than a guarantee of quality. I am not saying that all imported olive oils have been tampered with, but it's a good idea to buy your oil from reputable importers who have good relationships with artisan producers, even if it's more expensive.

If you're interested in learning more about olive oil, you should check out Tom Mueller's *Extra Virginity: The Sublime and Scandalous World of Olive Oil*. It's a quick yet engrossing read about the history of olive oil fraud and the producers, chefs, and food activists who are struggling to right the industry.

ITALIAN DRESSING

If you like the flavor of commercial Italian dressings, you may prefer to use a mild-flavored oil like canola instead of olive oil. Adding a little sugar and/or Parmigiano-Reggiano cheese is optional.

Yield: 1 1/3 cups (315 ml)

Ingredients

1/4 cup (60 ml) white wine vinegar

2 tablespoons (28 ml) lemon juice

1 tablespoon (15 ml) water

2 tablespoons (18 g) minced
  red bell pepper *(see page 121)*

3/4 teaspoon minced garlic or garlic purée
  (see page 17) or 1/4 teaspoon garlic powder

2 teaspoons grated onion *(see page 18)*
  or 1/2 teaspoon onion powder

3/4 teaspoon dried oregano

1/2 teaspoon ground fennel seed
  or 1/4 teaspoon fennel pollen *(see Note)*

1 teaspoon sugar *(optional)*

1 teaspoon sea salt or kosher salt

1/4 teaspoon freshly ground black pepper

3/4 cup (175 ml) extra-virgin olive oil
  or canola oil

2 tablespoons (10 g) grated Parmigiano-
  Reggiano or Parmesan cheese *(optional)*

Directions

In a small mixing bowl, whisk together the white wine vinegar, lemon juice, water, red bell pepper, garlic, onion, oregano, fennel, sugar, salt, and pepper. Let stand for 15 minutes.

After the herbs have begun to soften and rehydrate, whisk in the oil. Add the Parmigiano-Reggiano and whisk to combine. Serve. Store any unused portion, covered, in the refrigerator for up to 1 week.

Note: Fennel is very popular in Mediterranean food. It has a delicate flavor—light and sweet, similar to that of anise. Whole or ground fennel seed is used in sauces from marinara to pizza, and it's what gives sweet Italian sausage its distinct flavor.

Fennel pollen is made from fennel flowers harvested at full bloom. The flowers are dried and then the pollen is sifted out. The result is a delicately textured seasoning with intense flavor and aroma. I usually use about half the amount of fennel pollen as I would ground fennel. I like to sprinkle a little on roasted beets and goat cheese. I also recommend trying a dash on halibut or sea bass before roasting.

Variation: Red Italian—Add 2 tablespoons (30 g) of your favorite marinara sauce to the herb mixture. Whisk in the oil, but omit the Parmigiano-Reggiano.

Parmigiano–Reggiano vs. Parmesan: What's the difference?

Although you may think Parmesan is the English translation of Parmigiano-Reggiano, it's not quite that simple. Parmigiano-Reggiano is a DOC product (*Denominazione di Origine Controllata*), meaning it is regulated by Italian law, must come from certain provinces and regions in Italy, and must follow traditional artisan recipes. It's similar to Champagne. In order to be labeled Champagne, it must come from the Champagne region of France and follow traditional production methods. Although Parmesan is similar to its Italian cousin, it's sometimes lower quality and often less flavorful.

Purists will tell you that there is nothing like a true Parmigiano-Reggiano, and I'm inclined to agree with them. If you taste the two side by side, the differences will be quite evident. A good Parmigiano-

Reggiano is typically aged at least 2 years. It has amazing depth of flavor, ranging from nutty or grassy to sweet, fruity, and creamy. There's textural difference, too: Parmigiano-Reggiano has a granular crunch and a crystalline texture. Incidentally, that crunch doesn't come from salt. It's crystallized protein that forms during the aging process.

So, if you have an opportunity to try Parmigiano-Reggiano, I highly recommend it. And don't limit it to grating and shaving. It makes a wonderful addition to a cheese platter. I also save the rinds from my Parmigiano-Reggiano in the freezer to add to homemade soups, stews, and pasta sauces. You just drop a chunk into the pot when you are cooking. You can fish them out later and simply discard them or cut them into bite-size pieces and put them back into your soup or sauce.

MIX-AND-MATCH VINAIGRETTE

Don't get stuck in a rut when it comes to your vinaigrette. Think of it as an exercise in creativity!

A vinaigrette is a temporary emulsion sauce. Think of it as a flexible formula—typically **3 parts fat** (I know, I used a scary word but it's only because you are not limited to oil) to **1 part acid** (also might sound scary but it means you can think beyond vinegar). From there, you can add any number of **seasonings** and a **stabilizer** (the stuff that keeps it from separating as quickly).

Here are some ideas for each:

Fats
You can choose a neutral flavor like canola oil or a stronger flavor like olive oil or bacon fat.

Canola oil
Olive oil
Peanut oil
Walnut oil
Hazelnut oil
Grapeseed oil
Flavored or infused oils
Bacon fat
Heavy cream
Sour cream
Yogurt
Crème fraîche

Acids
Each of the following differs in flavor and level of acidity. You can adjust the fat-to-acid ratio accordingly. If something is strongly flavored, you may find the standard ratio is perfect. However, if it's more delicate and mildly flavored like rice vinegar or lime juice, you may want to increase the acid—more like 2 parts fat to 1 part acid.

Red wine vinegar
White wine vinegar
Balsamic vinegar
Champagne vinegar
Rice vinegar
Sherry vinegar
Cider vinegar
Mead (honey) vinegar
Infused or flavored vinegars
Citrus juices—lime, lemon, orange, or grapefruit
Verjus
Wine

Seasonings

Seasonings' sole purpose is to add flavor and aromas to your vinaigrette. If you are using dried herbs and spices, you might want to let your dressing rest for up to 1 hour before serving so that the seasonings have a chance to soften and release their essences.

Shallots
Onions—red, white, yellow, or sweet
Scallions
Garlic
Cheeses—from Parmigiano-Reggiano
  to crumbled blue cheese
Fresh herbs
Dried herbs
Ground spices
Jams and jellies
Salt—try different sea salts
  for texture and flavor
Chutneys
Pickles and relishes
Capers
Olives
Bacon or pancetta crumbles
Sesame oil

Stabilizers (Optional)

Stabilizers are also called emulsifiers. They help slow down the separation of acid and fat. They can also add flavor.

Mustard
Egg yolks
Pomegranate molasses
Dairy products—yogurt, sour cream,
  heavy cream, crème fraîche, and soft
  cheeses like goat chèvre can be used
  in conjunction with another fat to
  stabilize the vinaigrette
Roasted garlic or garlic purée
Vegetable purées
Fruit butters and purées
Stocks and broths

CAESAR SALAD DRESSING

When I make Caesar salad dressing, I add finely grated Parmigiano-Reggiano when tossing it with the salad. If you add it too early, the dressing can become too thick to toss.

Yield: 2/3 cup (160 ml)

Ingredients

2 eggs, the freshest you can find *(see page 12)*

1 1/2 teaspoons garlic purée *(see page 17)* or 1/4 rounded teaspoon garlic powder

1/4 teaspoon kosher salt or sea salt

2 to 4 teaspoons anchovy paste or mashed anchovies *(optional)*

1 teaspoon Dijon mustard *(see page 29)*

1/2 teaspoon Worcestershire sauce *(see page 36)*

1 tablespoon (15 ml) red wine vinegar *(page 70)* or garlic vinegar *(see page 75)*

2 tablespoons (28 ml) freshly squeezed lemon juice

1/2 teaspoon freshly ground pepper

1/3 cup (80 ml) extra-virgin olive oil

1/2 cup (50 g) grated Parmigiano-Reggiano or Parmesan, divided

Directions

Bring a small pot of water to a boil. Gently lower the eggs into the boiling water. Boil for 90 seconds and remove with a slotted spoon. Carefully crack them into a small bowl, being sure to scoop out the white that clings to the shell. Use a fork to beat the eggs slightly. Refrigerate until ready to use.

In a large salad bowl, combine the garlic purée, salt, anchovy paste, and mustard; mix to a smooth paste. Whisk in the Worcestershire sauce, vinegar, lemon juice, and black pepper. When the dressing base is fully blended, get the eggs out of the refrigerator. Slowly add the eggs to the dressing base, whisking constantly. Now, whisk in the olive oil. Mix until thick and smooth. Taste for salt and add more if necessary.

When you are about to toss your dressing with your salad, place the romaine lettuce in the bowl with the dressing. Toss until the leaves are evenly coated with dressing. Then add 1/4 cup (25 g) of the grated Parmigiano-Reggiano and toss again to blend. Serve the remaining 1/4 cup (25 g) grated cheese on the salad as garnish, along with croutons, if desired.

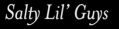

Salty Lil' Guys

Anchovies are one of the foods that are likely to make people cringe at the thought of them. These oily, little silver fish don't get nearly the respect they deserve. Before you pooh-pooh them, you might not realize that they are commonly used in some all-time favorites like Worcestershire sauce, Caesar salad, and green goddess dressing. Anchovies provide savory depth of flavor—the "something" you can't quite name. Foodies call it "umami," the fifth taste beyond sweet, salty, sour, and bitter. You're getting a little more interested, aren't you?

Okay, then, let's talk anchovies. First, although it's tempting to save money, anchovies are another example of getting what you pay for. The cheap ones often taste awful—probably what has contributed to the bad reputation. Anchovies are most commonly sold in cans, filleted and packed in oil. Try to purchase anchovies that are packed in olive oil for the best flavor.

If you don't mind a little extra work, you can purchase whole, salt-packed anchovies. You have to fillet them yourself but they are usually better quality.

Here are some hints: Don't be tempted by bargain-priced anchovies. The really good ones are never cheap, and the cheap ones are more likely to be really awful.

Always taste the anchovies when you open a can. If they taste too salty, rinse the ones you plan to use in a little warm water and pat them dry with a paper towel.

If the anchovies are packed in oil, pour it off and discard it. It will probably be too fishy or salty to use for anything else.

If you have leftover oil-packed anchovies, roll the fillets into circles and place them in a small airtight container. Cover them with extra-virgin olive oil. Then seal the container and store it in the refrigerator. Typically, you can store them in the refrigerator for 3 to 6 months.

If you have leftover salt-packed anchovies, remove them from the can and place them in a glass container. Cover the container and refrigerate them for up to 6 months.

If you don't want to work with anchovy fillets, try using anchovy paste. Anchovy paste is typically a blend of ground anchovies, salt, and oil. Some pastes include a little sugar to mellow the flavor. I keep a tube in the refrigerator to use for salad dressings, dips, and pasta sauces. You can store the tube in your refrigerator for 6 months, but always follow the manufacturer's "best by" recommendations.

BUTTERMILK RANCH DRESSING

I'm really picky about ranch dressing. The bottled brands just taste synthetic to me. Once you taste this tangy, herby dressing you'll feel the same.

Yield: 1 1/4 cups (295 ml)

Ingredients

1/3 cup (77 g) sour cream
   or crème fraîche *(see sidebar)*

1/3 cup (75 g) mayonnaise *(see page 10)*

1/2 cup (120 ml) buttermilk

1 1/2 teaspoons fresh lemon juice
   or white wine vinegar

2 teaspoons grated onion *(see page 18)*
   or 1/2 teaspoon onion powder

1/2 teaspoon garlic purée *(see page 17)*
   or pinch of garlic powder

1 1/2 teaspoons minced fresh chives

1 1/2 teaspoons minced fresh
   parsley *(see page 14)*

Pinch of dried thyme

Pinch of paprika

3/4 teaspoon kosher salt or sea salt

Freshly ground black pepper to taste

Directions

Whisk the sour cream, mayonnaise, and buttermilk together until smooth and fully blended. Stir in the lemon juice, onion, garlic, chives, parsley, thyme, and paprika. Season with salt and a generous grinding of pepper. Refrigerate, covered, until ready to use. Store in the refrigerator for up to 3 days.

Note: The flavors of this dressing improve with a little time. If you can, try to make the recipe at least 1 hour before you plan to serve it. Refrigerate until ready to use.

Get a Little Culture—Crème Fraîche

If you left a glass of milk on the counter overnight, you probably wouldn't want to drink it in the morning, right? We have a tendency to get a little freaked out about bacteria—rightly so in some cases, but in others a little bit of bacteria is a good thing.

Crème fraîche (French for "fresh cream") is cultured cream, not just because it has a fancy French name, but rather because it's thickened by bacterial cultures. It can range in thickness from heavy whipping cream to sour cream.

It's very simple to make. In a small nonre- active mixing bowl, add 1 tablespoon (15 ml) buttermilk to 1 cup (235 ml) heavy

cream. Stir to combine. Cover and let rest for 12 to 24 hours at room temperature. The longer you wait, the thicker it will become. When the crème fraîche reaches the desired thickness, refrigerate it for at least 24 hours before using. The finished crème fraîche can be stored in the refrig- erator for up to 10 days.

Crème fraîche is slightly less sour than sour cream, so it can be used for all sorts of dressings, sauces, and desserts. It's delicious plain, but you can add fresh herbs and lemon juice for an herbed cream sauce. Or add a little sugar and vanilla and spoon it over fresh berries.

BLUE CHEESE DRESSING

This is a thick, creamy, tangy, pass-a-wedge-of-iceberg dressing! Okay, I'd settle for a platter of Buffalo wings in a pinch.

Yield: 1 1/2 cups (355 ml)

Ingredients

4 ounces (115 g) blue cheese, crumbled *(see sidebar)*

1/2 teaspoon kosher salt or sea salt

1/2 teaspoon freshly ground black pepper, or more to taste

1 teaspoon grated onion *(see page 18)* or rounded 1/4 teaspoon onion powder

1 1/2 teaspoons garlic purée *(see page 17)* or 1/4 teaspoon garlic powder

1/4 teaspoon dry ground mustard

1/2 cup (115 g) sour cream or crème fraîche *(see page 87)*

1/3 cup (75 g) mayonnaise *(see page 10)*

1/2 cup (120 ml) buttermilk

1 tablespoon (15 ml) white wine vinegar

1 tablespoon (3 g) finely chopped chives

Directions

In a medium-size bowl, crumble the blue cheese and add the salt and pepper. Use a fork to break up the blue cheese into small crumbles.

Stir in the onion, garlic, mustard, sour cream, mayonnaise, buttermilk, and vinegar until well mixed. Try a taste and decide if you'd like a little more salt or pepper. Garnish with a sprinkle of chives. At this point, the dressing will be a bit runny. If you prefer a thicker dressing, refrigerate overnight before using.

This dressing becomes more flavorful over time. You can also store it in the refrigerator, covered, for up to 3 days.

Am I Blue or Bleu?

When I was a little girl, they still spelled bleu cheese the French way on most menus, and I thought Roquefort was the best. Over the years, the spelling has become Anglicized and the variety of blue cheeses available has expanded quite a bit. I thought it might be helpful to give you an overview of a few popular varieties.

The term blue cheese refers to the presence of mold throughout the cheese. That mold gives the cheese its streaky blue/green-veined appearance and influences the flavor. Originally, mold developed naturally in the cheeses while they were cave-aged. Today, mold is typically injected into the cheese or added to the curds for even distribution. The longer a cheese ages, the more intense the flavor becomes. Although traditional Roquefort is made from sheep's milk, blue cheeses are also made from cow or goat's milk. I've listed several common varieties, along with general descriptions of flavor.

Danish Blue (Danablu)—Developed in the 1900s in Denmark, Danish blue is a relatively mild and creamy cow's milk cheese.

Roquefort—Made from sheep's milk, Roquefort is one of France's national treasures. This cave-aged cheese has a slightly porous texture with blue-green streaks. It has a soft, creamy texture and a spicy taste.

Stilton—Considered to be the king of English cheeses, Stilton is manufactured from sheep or cow's milk. It has a tangy acidity and a crumbly texture.

Maytag—Created in the 1940s by the grandsons of the founder of Maytag appliances, this cow's milk blue was modeled after Roquefort. It has a creamy, pungent flavor and a slightly crumbly consistency.

Gorgonzola—Named for a small city outside of Milan, this blue can be made from either cow's or goat's milk. It comes in two textures: soft (Gorgonzola dolce) and aged, crumbly-firm (Gorgonzola picante). I typically select the Gorgonzola picante for dressing. It has a nice salty, sharp taste.

GREEN GODDESS DRESSING

I love goddess dressing, with its salty, herbaceous tang.
As a child, I had no idea that the saltiness came from the dreaded
anchovy! My advice to you is to serve the dressing and don't
mention the anchovies.

Yield: 1 3/4 cups (410 ml)

Ingredients

1 cup (225 g) mayonnaise *(see page 10)*

1 tablespoon (16 g) anchovy paste
  or mashed anchovy fillets

3 tablespoons (9 g) minced chives
  or (18 g) scallions

2 tablespoons (8 g) minced parsley *(see page 14)*

1/2 teaspoon garlic purée *(see page 17)*
  or pinch of garlic powder

1 tablespoon (15 ml) freshly
  squeezed lemon juice

3 tablespoons (45 ml) chive blossom vinegar
  (see page 72) or tarragon vinegar *(see page 74)*

1/2 cup (120 ml) heavy cream

Sea salt or kosher salt to taste

Freshly ground black pepper to taste

Directions

Put all the ingredients in a medium-size
mixing bowl or blender. Whisk vigorously
until smooth and fully blended or process
in the blender for 20 to 30 seconds.
Refrigerate for at least 30 minutes prior
to serving to enhance the flavor.

POPPY SEED DRESSING

Poppy seed dressing was one that rarely occurred to me
to make from scratch. That is, until I figured out how simple
it was! Try this dressing on a spinach salad with sliced mushrooms,
crumbled bacon, chopped egg, and raisins. You can also toss
in some orange segments. Yum!

Yield: 1 1/2 cups (355 ml)

Ingredients

1/3 (67 g) granulated sugar

1/2 cup (120 ml) white wine vinegar

1 1/4 teaspoons kosher salt or sea salt

1 teaspoon dry mustard powder

1 teaspoon grated onion *(see page 18)*
   or 1/4 rounded teaspoon onion powder

1 cup (235 ml) rice bran oil or canola oil

1 tablespoon (9 g) poppy seeds

Directions

Combine the sugar and vinegar in a small saucepan. Heat over medium-low heat, stirring occasionally, until the sugar has dissolved, about 3 minutes. Remove the pan from the heat and whisk in the salt and mustard powder. Allow to cool for 15 minutes.

When the spiced vinegar has reached room temperature, pour the mixture into a blender or food processor and add the onion. Process for 20 seconds to incorporate. Then, with the blender or food processor on high, gradually add the oil in a slow, steady stream. Process until the oil is fully incorporated and the dressing is smooth, about 3 minutes. Add the poppy seeds and process to combine, about 10 seconds.

Allow the dressing to rest at room temperature for at least 15 minutes or refrigerate to chill. Add more salt, if desired. Store unused dressing, covered, in the refrigerator for up to 2 weeks.

HONEY MUSTARD DRESSING

This dressing is versatile enough to use on salads or as a dip.

Yield: 1 cup (235 ml)

Ingredients

1/2 cup (160 g) honey

1/4 cup (44 g) Dijon mustard *(see page 29)*

2 tablespoons (28 ml) cider vinegar
   or balsamic vinegar

Kosher salt or sea salt and freshly
   ground pepper to taste

Directions

Combine all the ingredients in a bowl
and whisk until smooth. Taste and add
salt and pepper if desired. Serve. Store
covered, in the refrigerator, for up
to 3 months.

Note: Honey, mustard, and vinegar are
almost the trifecta of everlasting ingredients, so this dressing has a great shelf
(refrigerator) life.

Variations: Orange Honey Mustard—
Add 1 tablespoon (6 g) finely grated
orange zest.

Creamy Honey Mustard—Add 1/2 cup
(115 g) mayonnaise *(see page 10)* to the
dressing and whisk until thoroughly
combined. Adding mayonnaise reduces
the shelf (refrigerator) life of the dressing.
Store, covered, for up to 3 days in
the refrigerator.

FRENCH DRESSING

When I was a little girl, I'd often see bright orangey-red Catalina dressings (aka Catalina French dressing) on salad bars in the Midwest. My dad used to drizzle a little on top of his blue cheese-dressed salads. Trust me, he's got something there.

Yield: 2 1/2 cups (570 ml)

Ingredients

3/4 cup (150 g) sugar

2 teaspoons coarse sea salt or kosher salt

Dash of paprika

1/2 teaspoon celery seed

1/2 teaspoon dry mustard powder

1 teaspoon grated onion *(see page 18)* or 1/4 teaspoon onion powder

1 teaspoon Worcestershire sauce *(see page 36)*

1/2 cup (120 ml) cider vinegar

1/2 cup (120 g) ketchup *(see page 30)*

1 cup (235 ml) canola oil or rice bran oil

Directions

In a medium saucepan, combine the sugar, salt, paprika, celery seed, mustard, grated onion, Worcestershire, and vinegar. Warm over medium-low heat until the sugar dissolves and all the ingredients have blended. Stir in the ketchup and mix thoroughly.

Remove from the heat and whisk in the oil. When the dressing is smooth, transfer to the refrigerator to chill for 1 hour. Serve. Store unused dressing in the refrigerator for up to 2 weeks.

Variation: **Creamy French**—Add 1/2 cup (115 g) mayonnaise to the dressing and whisk or blenderize to combine. If you prepare the Creamy French Dressing using homemade mayonnaise, you can store the unused dressing in the refrigerator for up to 3 days. If you use store-bought mayonnaise, you can store any unused dressing in the refrigerator for up to 1 week.

THOUSAND ISLAND DRESSING

Did you know that Americans spend $200,000,000 on Thousand Island dressing each year?

Yield: 1 1/2 cups (355 ml)

Ingredients

1 cup (225 g) mayonnaise *(see page 10)*

3 tablespoons (60 g) chili sauce *(see page 35)* or ketchup *(see page 30)*

1 1/2 teaspoons cider vinegar

1 tablespoon (9 g) finely chopped green bell pepper

1 tablespoon (12 g) finely chopped pimento

2 tablespoons (18 g) finely chopped hard-boiled egg *(optional)*

1 1/2 teaspoons minced onion

Sea salt or kosher salt to taste

Freshly ground black pepper to taste

Directions

Put all the ingredients in a medium-size mixing bowl or blender. Whisk vigorously until smooth and fully blended or process in the blender for 20 to 30 seconds. Refrigerate for at least 30 minutes prior to serving to enhance the flavor.

Variation: **Relish Thousand Island**—Omit the green bell pepper and pimento and add sweet pickle relish *(see page 120)*.

COLESLAW DRESSING

This coleslaw dressing is sweet, tangy,
and creamy—absolute perfection.

*Yield: 1 1/2 cups (355 ml), enough for 1
pound (455 g) of cabbage*

Ingredients

1 cup (225 g) mayonnaise *(see page 10)*

2 tablespoons (22 g) Dijon mustard *(see page 29)*
  or whole-grain mustard *(see page 27)*

1/3 cup (67 g) sugar

2 tablespoons (28 ml) cider vinegar

1 tablespoon (10 g) grated onion *(see page 18)*
  or 3/4 teaspoon onion powder

2 teaspoons celery seed

1/2 teaspoon sea salt or kosher salt,
  plus more, to taste

Pinch of freshly ground black pepper

Directions

Combine all the ingredients in a small
mixing bowl. Stir until smooth and fully
blended. Chill until ready to use.

Serving Suggestion

Pour the dressing over 1 pound (455 g)
finely chopped or shredded green
cabbage. Refrigerate for a minimum
of 2 hours or overnight. Here are some
coleslaw additions:

Use 1/2 pound (225 g) each of purple
  cabbage and green cabbage

Add 1 medium-size grated carrot

Add 1/3 cup (50 g) finely diced bell
  pepper *(see page 121)*

Add 1 small apple, peeled and finely
  diced, and 1/4 cup (36 g) raisins

Add 1/2 cup (120 g) crushed
  or (80 g) diced pineapple

Add 1/4 cup (28 g) chopped pecans

SESAME TAHINI DRESSING

The sesame oil and tahini add toasty balance to this light,
Asian-style dressing.

Yield: 3/4 cup (175 ml)

Ingredients

2 tablespoons (28 ml) rice vinegar
  or cider vinegar

2 teaspoons freshly squeezed lemon juice

1 tablespoon (10 g) minced shallot

2 teaspoons sugar

1/2 teaspoon sea salt or kosher salt

Pinch of ground white pepper

3 tablespoons (45 g) tahini *(see page 53)*

2 tablespoons (28 ml) toasted sesame oil

6 tablespoons (90 ml) rice bran oil
  or canola oil

1 1/2 teaspoons sesame seeds

Thinly sliced scallions, for garnish *(optional)*

Directions

In a small mixing bowl, combine the rice
vinegar, lemon juice, shallot, sugar, salt,
and white pepper. Whisk until the sugar
and salt have dissolved. Let the flavors
infuse for 10 to 15 minutes.

Next, add the tahini and whisk until smooth
and creamy. Now whisk in the sesame
oil and rice bran oil. When the oils are
thoroughly blended, stir in the sesame
seeds. Taste to see if you would like to
add more salt and pepper. Garnish with
the sliced scallions and serve. Refrigerate
any unused portion for up to 1 week
in a covered container.

Note: The flavors of this dressing increase
and blend with a little time. If you can,
let the dressing rest for at least 1 hour
before serving. If the oil separates a bit,
whisk to blend.

ASIAN GINGER DRESSING

This dressing has zing! It's perfect with a salad of baby greens, chicken, and cashews.

Yield: 1 1/4 cups (295 ml)

Ingredients

1 teaspoon minced garlic

2 tablespoons (12 g) minced
   fresh ginger root

1 tablespoon (10 g) minced shallot

1 tablespoon (15 ml) wheat-free tamari
   or soy sauce

1/3 cup (80 ml) rice vinegar
   or cider vinegar

3 tablespoons (60 g) honey

3/4 cup (180 ml) rice bran oil
   or peanut oil

1 tablespoon (15 ml) sesame oil

Sea salt or kosher salt, to taste

Pinch of ground white pepper

Directions

In a medium-size mixing bowl, whisk together the garlic, ginger, shallot, tamari, and vinegar. Allow to rest for 15 minutes to infuse the flavors.

Next, add the honey and whisk until fully dissolved in the vinegar. When the honey has been incorporated, whisk in the rice bran oil and sesame oil. Season to taste with salt and pepper.

The flavors of this dressing improve with time. If you have time, allow it to steep for 1 hour at room temperature. Whisk to blend again prior to serving. Store, covered, in the refrigerator for up to 1 week.

CHAPTER FOUR: STOCKS

"STOCK TO A COOK IS LIKE VOICE TO A SINGER."

— *Anonymous*

The quote for this chapter could well have been, "Waste not, want not." Using bones and vegetable scraps you might otherwise throw away is responsible, economical, and rewarding. On top of that, making stock from scratch is far more healthful than using canned broth, and the flavor can't be beat. Once you've gotten into the habit of making and using your own stock, you'll balk at the idea of canned broth.

What I want you to understand most about stocks is that you aren't making soup. You are making the base for soup or sauce. Stock, as a chef uses it, is an ingredient, in the same way eggs are to egg salad or a cake. Using homemade stock will make your dishes sing!

IN STOCK—THE OVERVIEW

Stock making is a simple process, but there are a few tips
that can refine your technique and improve the final result.

On the Pot
You might refer to any large pot as
a stockpot, but in actuality a stockpot
should be taller than it is wide, with high,
straight sides and two loop handles. Taller
versus wider is very important when it comes
to simmering stock over many hours
because less steam escapes—less surface
area exposed equals more stock in the
pot when you are done. The loop handles
make it easier to move a heavy liquid-
filled pot. Some stockpots have a spigot
at the bottom edge that allows you to
drain the liquid without picking up the
pot—very handy but not necessary for
most home cooks.

Are We Clear?
Starting with cold water helps ensure
that the finished stock will be clear
instead of cloudy. Adding cold water
causes the fat, blood, and other impurities
to dissolve more slowly. As the water
heats, the impurities coagulate and float
to the surface to be skimmed away.
Starting with warm water causes the
impurities to dissolve too quickly and
cloud the stock instead of floating to the
surface. Skimming the stock, especially
during the first hour, helps remove impurities that can also result in cloudy broth.
You don't want a murky stock, especially
for clear soups like chicken noodle.
A properly made stock will glisten.

Another important tip: don't overheat
the stock. Once you've brought the stock
to a boil, reduce the heat immediately
to a gentle simmer. Over-boiling leads to
cloudy stock, too.

The Power of the Peel
If you get into the habit of making stock,
here's a good tip: save carrot peels, onion
skins, stems and roots, and celery leaves
and hearts, instead of throwing them away.
Although you may not eat them, they
are perfect to use in stock making. As
a matter of fact, many professional kitchens
do the same. Peels and leaves impart flavor
and would otherwise become compost
or landfill. Save them in a container in
your refrigerator and use them along
with the diced vegetables in the recipe.
You can keep them refrigerated for up
to two weeks. It makes me feel good to
use something that might otherwise be
tossed away!

By the way, it is not necessary to peel
the vegetables you chop for stock. Just
make sure that they are clean.

The Role of the Dice

Learning standard sizes for dicing is helpful because it eliminates confusion in interpreting recipes. When making stock, you must consider how long you'll be cooking the liquid and how much time it takes to impart flavor from the ingredients. For example, when you are making a quick-cooking stock like fish stock or court bouillon, use a small dice so that the vegetables cook quickly and add flavor to the liquid in a short amount of time. With a longer-cooking stock like a beef stock, vegetables should be larger so they don't completely disintegrate over many hours of cooking.

If a recipe calls for a small dice, that means chopping vegetables into some approximation of ¼-inch (6 mm) square, for medium try ½-inch (1.3 cm) square, and for large cut ¾-inch (2 cm) square. You don't need to be perfect, just aim for relative consistency. It takes practice, so don't be too hard on yourself.

Sachet-ing Around
A sachet d'epices is a classic combination of spices, including parsley stems, bay leaf, thyme, and black pepper, all tied up in a square of cheesecloth. The combo is commonly used in stock making. The idea behind a bundle is to make it easy to fish out of the stock at the end of the cooking process. Frankly, it's a bit fussy for me. I follow the advice of my friend and fellow chef, Jean-Marie Rigollet, and just add the spices directly to the stock. They infuse more flavor while mingling freely in the liquid, and you'll be straining the stock when it's finished anyway.

Salt Away
When you taste canned commercial broth, unless it's low sodium, it probably tastes like soup without the vegetables. That's because we're used to salt creating the flavor. True stock, like they use in professional kitchens, doesn't include salt. That's because professional chefs think of stock as an ingredient instead of a final product. They add salt to the finished dishes—soups, gravies, risottos, etc. That way, they control the flavor all the way through the cooking process. The flavor of stock is richer and deeper than broth, and as you learn to cook with it, you'll grow to appreciate it more and more.

CHICKEN STOCK

Save your leftover chicken bones in the freezer until
you've accumulated enough to make stock. Chicken stock
is a great ingredient to keep on hand because it's so versatile.
Use it for soups, braising vegetables, cooking rice
and other grains, and making gravy.

Yield: About 3 quarts (2.8 L)

Ingredients

4 pounds (1.8 kg) chicken bones,
   roasted or raw

1 gallon (3.8 L) cold water

1 1/2 cups (240 g) medium-diced onion

3/4 cup (98 g) medium-diced carrot

3/4 cup (75 g) medium-diced celery

1 bay leaf

Pinch of dried thyme

4 whole black peppercorns

2 parsley stems, leaves removed,
   or 1 teaspoon dried parsley

Directions

Place the chicken bones in a large stockpot. Add the cold water. Make sure the bones are completely covered; if not, add a bit more water.

Bring the water to a boil. Reduce the heat and simmer the bones for 1 hour. Foam will begin to rise to the surface of the water. Skim it away using a skimmer or large spoon as it accumulates, about every 15 minutes for that first hour.

Add the remaining ingredients to the pot. Return the water to a simmer and cook for 5 to 6 hours. Do not stir during this time.

Cut a piece of cheesecloth large enough to line a sieve. Moisten the cheesecloth under running water, and then squeeze it to remove the excess moisture. Line the sieve with the moist cheesecloth. (Moistening the cheesecloth removes loose fibers and helps the cloth adhere to the sieve.) Place the lined sieve over a large bowl or pot.

Create an ice bath in your kitchen sink. Fill the sink basin about one-fourth full with cold water and add ice until the sink is half full.

Use a large slotted spoon to remove the bones and vegetables. Discard. After you have removed most of the debris, pour the stock through the lined sieve into the large bowl. Place the bowl of strained stock into the ice bath. Allow the stock to cool completely. Stir from time to time to speed the cooling process.

Pour the cooled stock into resealable container(s) and refrigerate. Overnight, a layer of fat will form across the surface of the stock. Simply peel it away to access the stock below.

Your stock can be refrigerated for up to 7 days. You can also freeze your stock for up to 3 months. To freeze, divide the stock among small containers—1 to 4 cups (235 to 950 ml) per container. Refrigerate overnight, then remove the layer of fat, cover the container, and freeze.

Note: You can use the poultry fat from the top of the stock to sauté potatoes or vegetables. Or try rubbing a little melted poultry fat on the skin of a whole chicken before you roast it. Just like rubbing the

skin with butter or layering a little bacon, the poultry fat helps seal in moisture and crisp the skin. I store my poultry fat in the freezer in zip-top bags. When I need a piece, I simply cut off the amount I plan to use and melt it in the pan.

TIP: It's a good idea to identify your containers or you can end up with a mystery box at the back of the freezer. Really, stocks look a lot alike. I use a piece of masking tape and a marker to identify which type of stock I have and when I made it.

BEEF STOCK

Good-quality stock is high in minerals and contains virtually no sodium. You can add salt to taste when you are cooking with it.

Yield: About 3 quarts (2.8 L)

Ingredients

6 pounds (2.7 kg) veal or beef bones *(see Note)*

1 1/2 gallons (5.7 L) cold water

3 cups (480 g) large-diced onion, peels and all

1 1/2 cups (195 g) large-diced carrots, peels and all

1 1/2 cups (150 g) 3/4-inch (2 cm) chunks celery, leaves and all

2 bay leaves

12 whole black peppercorns

1/8 teaspoon dried thyme

4 parsley stems or 2 teaspoons dried parsley

1/4 cup (60 ml) red wine vinegar *(see page 70)*

Directions

Place the veal bones in a large stockpot. Add the cold water. Make sure the bones are completely covered; if not, add a bit more water. Place the pot on the stove over high heat. Bring to a boil and then reduce the heat and simmer the bones for 1 hour. Skim away any foam that forms on the surface of the water. The foam contains impurities and can influence the flavor and clarity of the stock if you don't

remove it. You will probably need to skim the foam about 4 times during the first hour. After that, the foaming should subside.

After 1 hour, add the remaining ingredients and continue to simmer for 12 to 24 hours. I know this seems like a very long time, but unlike chicken bones, veal bones are quite thick and so it takes time to render the flavor and minerals from them. The vinegar helps extract the minerals from the bones as well. I usually let my beef stock simmer the full 24 hours. Do not stir the stock while it's cooking.

When the stock is finished simmering, use tongs to remove the bones. Use a slotted spoon to remove most of the smaller bones and vegetables. Discard.

Cut a piece of cheesecloth large enough to line a sieve. Moisten the cheesecloth under running water and then squeeze it to remove the excess moisture. Line the sieve with the moist cheesecloth. (Moistening the cheesecloth removes loose fibers and helps the cloth adhere to the sieve.) Place the lined sieve over a large bowl or pot. Create an ice bath in your kitchen sink. Fill the sink basin about one-fourth full with cold water and add ice until the sink is half full.

Pour the liquid through the sieve to strain. Place the bowl of strained stock into the ice bath. Allow the stock to cool completely. Stir from time to time to speed the cooling process.

Pour the cooled stock into resealable container(s). Refrigerate for up to 7 days. A layer of fat will form on top of the chilled stock. It's kind of a natural seal. Simply crack and remove it to use the stock.

You can also freeze your stock for up to 3 months. To freeze, divide the stock among small containers—1 to 4 cups (235 to 950 ml) per container. Refrigerate overnight, then remove the layer of fat, cover the container, and freeze.

It's a good idea to mark and date your containers. You may think you'll remember what that container is filled with and when you made it, but if I don't identify it with a piece of masking tape, I am likely to forget.

Note: Veal bones make the best stock because they are softer, so the minerals and collagen can be more easily extracted during the cooking process. If you can't find veal bones at your local grocery store, you can substitute beef bones, including oxtails, neck bones, and short ribs. Ideally, the bones should be cut into sections no longer than 3 to 4 inches (7.5 to 10 cm). If they are bigger than that, I suggest cooking them for the full 24 hours to get the most flavor and nutrients from them.

Healthy Benefits

You might ask yourself, "Why make stock when I can buy broth in the grocery store?" For me there are two answers to this question. Number one, homemade stock is far superior to canned broth. Most of the flavor in canned broth comes from salt. Homemade stock is richer and more flavorful, with almost no sodium. You control the amount of salt when you use the stock to make soup, sauce, gravy, risotto, or whatever. Number two, homemade stock is made from bones as opposed to canned broth, which can be made from meat scraps. Stock made from bones is rich in calcium, magnesium, phosphorus, and other trace minerals. It also contains gelatin, which aids in digestion and has been used in the treatment of many intestinal disorders such as hyperacidity, colitis, and Crohn's disease. A healthy digestive system supports the immune system, too. So, the idea of serving chicken soup for a cold has some merit.

CHICKEN GLACE

Chicken glace, aka *glace de poulet*, can be used in place of chicken bouillon. It's basically super-stock: stock reduced to a syrupy glaze.

Two tablespoons (28 ml) of glace added to 1 cup (235 ml) of water equals 1 cup (235 ml) of stock. You can also add glace cubes directly to soups, sauces, or gravies for a flavor boost.

Yield: About 16 tablespoons (235 ml)

Ingredients

8 cups (1.9 L) homemade
  chicken stock *(see page 104)* *(see Note)*

Directions

Pour the chicken stock into a medium-size stockpot. Bring the stock to a boil over high heat. If any foam forms on top of the stock, skim it away. Lower the heat and simmer until the stock is reduced by one-quarter (the remaining stock should be around 6 cups [1.4 L]). Continue to skim any foam that appears. Remove the reduced stock from the heat.

Line a fine-mesh sieve with cheesecloth. Place the sieve over a medium-size saucepan. Pour the stock through the lined sieve into the saucepan.

Place the saucepan back onto the stovetop. Bring the contents to a boil over high heat again. Reduce the heat and continue to simmer the stock. When the stock has reduced to 1 cup (235 ml), it should be thick and syrupy. It should take about 2 to 3 hours to reduce completely. The natural collagen in the bones will give it body and thickness.

Cool the glace slightly and then measure 1-tablespoon (15 ml) portions into an ice cube tray. Refrigerate or freeze until solid and then pop the tablespoon-size (15 ml) cubes out of the tray.

You can also pour the glace into a small square container (about 4 x 4 inches [10 x 10 cm]) lined with plastic wrap. Refrigerate the glace until solid. Use the plastic wrap to pull the glace out of the container. Remove the plastic wrap and then slice the glace into cubes.

Store the glace cubes in a plastic bag or an airtight container in the freezer for up to 3 months.

Note: Make sure you make this recipe with homemade chicken stock rather than commercial broth or stock. If not, the resulting glace will be runny and so salty you won't be able to use it.

BEEF GLACE

Beef glace, aka *glace de viande*, makes the richest sauce imaginable. You can also use it to make soups and stews.

Two tablespoons (28 ml) of glace added to 1 cup (235 ml) of water equals 1 cup (235 ml) of stock. It takes up less room in your freezer than stock, so it's nice to have on hand.

Yield: About 16 tablespoons (235 ml)

Ingredients

8 cups (1.9 L) homemade beef stock *(see page 106)*, refrigerated *(see Note)*

Directions

Remove the fat layer from the top of the beef stock. (Beef fat makes marvelous french fries and potato chips, so you can refrigerate it to use later or simply discard it.)

Spoon or pour the stock into a medium-size stockpot. Bring the stock to a boil over high heat. If any foam forms on top of the stock, skim it away using a skimmer or large spoon. Watch the pot closely while the foaming occurs; sometimes it will overflow. Lower the heat and simmer until the stock is reduced to a thick brown syrup. This will take 2 to 3 hours depending on the heat setting of your stove top. Keep an eye on the liquid so it doesn't boil away completely. You should have about 1 cup (235 ml) glace after it's reduced.

Cool the glace slightly and then measure 1-tablespoon (15 ml) portions into an ice cube tray. Refrigerate or freeze until solid and then pop the tablespoon-size cubes out of the tray.

If you don't have an ice cube tray, you can pour the glace into a small square container (about 4 x 4 inches [10 x 10 cm]) lined with plastic wrap. Refrigerate the glace until solid. Use the plastic wrap to pull the glace out of the container. Remove the plastic wrap and then slice the glace into cubes. Store the cubes a plastic bag or an airtight container in the freezer for up to 3 months.

Note: Make sure that you make this recipe with homemade beef stock rather than commercial broth or stock. If not, the resulting glace will be so salty you won't be able to use it.

Glace vs. Demi-Glace

You may be more familiar with the term *demi-glace*. Demi-glace, French for "half glaze," is actually a sauce made from equal parts brown stock (stock made from roasted veal or beef bones) and brown sauce (a classic sauce made from brown stock, thickened with tomatoes and roux). Glace, on the other hand, is simply stock that's been reduced to a syrupy consistency—no added thickening. Sometimes I see the terms used interchangeably, but technically they aren't the same.

VEGETABLE STOCK

It's important to note that this is not a vegetable soup, rather a stock that could be used to make soup. Traditional stocks don't include salt because they are an ingredient, like eggs or butter. You add salt to the final dish. This stock is a wonderful ingredient for vegetarian soups, risottos, and rice pilafs.

Yield: 8 cups (1.9 L)

Ingredients

2 tablespoons (28 g) unsalted butter

1/2 cup (80 g) thinly sliced onion

1 cup (84 g) thinly sliced leeks

1/4 cup (25 g) small-diced celery

1/3 cup (43 g) small-diced carrots

1/2 cup (90 g) small-diced tomato

2 cloves garlic, crushed

8 cups (1.9 L) cold water

2 parsley stems or 1 teaspoon dried parsley

1/4 teaspoon dried thyme

5 whole black peppercorns

1 bay leaf

1/2 teaspoon fennel seeds *(optional)*

1 whole clove

Directions

In a large, high-sided saucepan, melt the butter over medium heat. Add the vegetables and sweat them (cook them slowly, don't brown) until the onions become translucent and softened, about 10 minutes.

Add the water and spices. Bring to a boil, and then reduce the heat and simmer for 30 to 40 minutes.

Pour the stock through a fine-mesh strainer or cheesecloth-lined colander. Press the vegetables gently to extract all the stock. Let cool to room temperature and then pour into resealable containers and refrigerate for up to 1 week. Vegetable stock can also be frozen for up to 3 months.

Note: Vegetable stock sometimes includes other root vegetables like turnips or rutabagas. You can experiment by adding one or the other to this basic stock—1/4 cup (38 g) should be plenty. Or, for a more earthy taste, try adding 1 cup (70 g) chopped mushrooms.

Parsley Stems

You'll notice that I've listed parsley stems in most of the stock recipes in this chapter. The reason you would use parsley stems, as opposed to parsley leaves, is that stems impart flavor without color.

Aww Leek Out!

Leeks are members of the lily family like their cousins, onion and garlic. The long cylindrical bulbs are less commonly used in the United States than in Europe, but once you discover their delicate, oniony flavor, you'll want to incorporate them into your vegetable rotation. They are scrumptious in soups and stews, as well as braised or sautéed for a side dish.

Cleaning them properly is important. Sand and grit have a tendency to work their way between the layers. To clean them, first trim off the darkest green, thick sheaths at the top, leaving the whitish base and some of the paler green leaves intact. The dark green leaves are a bit too tough to eat, but you can certainly use them to flavor stock.

If you are planning to slice the leeks for soup or stock, you can cut them completely in half lengthwise and trim away the roots. However, if you are planning to braise the leeks as a side dish, it's nice to maintain the structure. So, rather than slice them completely in half lengthwise you can leave part of the root end in one piece. Use a sharp knife to slice lengthwise through the leek starting about 1 inch (2.5 cm) from the base of the root. Then trim off any stringy roots, being careful not to break apart the rest of the leek.

To wash away any grit that has nestled between the layers, you can soak the leeks in a cold water bath for 10 to 15 minutes. Next, hold the leek under cool running water and gently splay the layers to rinse any remaining residue. Pat the leeks dry and they're ready to use.

FISH STOCK

Fish stock is superb in chowders and stews.
It makes an outstanding stock for seafood risottos
that include scallops or shrimp, too.

Yield: 8 cups (1.9 L)

Ingredients

1 tablespoon (14 g) unsalted butter

1/3 cup (55 g) finely diced onion

2 parsley stems or 1 teaspoon dried parsley

2 1/2 pounds (1.1 kg) fish bones *(see Note)*
   and/or shrimp shells

3/4 cup (175 ml) dry white wine
   or dry sherry

1 tablespoon (15 ml) freshly
   squeezed lemon juice

8 cups (1.9 L) cold water

1/4 cup (18 g) finely chopped
   fresh mushrooms

Pinch of dried thyme

Directions

Melt the butter over medium heat in a medium-size stockpot. Add the onion, parsley, and fish bones. Cover the pot with a lid, reduce the heat to medium-low, and sweat the bones for 15 minutes. The onions should be translucent by this time.

Uncover the pot and add the wine and lemon juice. Stir the pot, scraping the bottom lightly to dislodge any stuck particles. Increase the heat to medium-high and simmer for 5 minutes.

Add the cold water, mushrooms, and thyme. Increase the heat to high and bring the stock to a boil. Reduce the heat and simmer the stock for 30 to 40 minutes. Skim any foam that rises to the surface with a skimmer or large spoon.

Cut a piece of cheesecloth large enough to line a sieve. Moisten the cheesecloth under running water and then squeeze it to remove the excess moisture. Line the sieve with the moist cheesecloth. (Moistening the cheesecloth removes loose fibers and helps the cloth adhere to the sieve.) Place the lined sieve over a large bowl or pot. Create an ice bath in your kitchen sink. Fill the sink basin about one-fourth full with cold water and add ice until the sink is half full.

Pour the stock through the sieve into a large bowl. Place the bowl in the ice bath to cool. Refrigerate the finished stock for up to 1 week.

Note: When choosing fish bones for stock, select bones from mild white fish like sole, cod, snapper, rockfish, or halibut. Avoid oily fish like salmon and mackerel. Strong-flavored, oily fish are too overpowering for stock.

COURT BOUILLON

More cooking liquid than stock, court bouillon is a fast,
aromatic broth used to poach fish, chicken, shellfish,
or vegetables. It's a nice way to infuse flavor.

Yield: 8 cups (1.9 L)

Ingredients

8 cups (1.9 L) cold water

1/3 cup (80 ml) white wine vinegar

2 tablespoons (28 ml) freshly
   squeezed lemon juice

1 cup (130 g) sliced carrots

1 cup (160 g) sliced onions

Pinch of dried thyme

1 bay leaf

5 parsley stems or 2 teaspoons
   dried parsley

4 whole black peppercorns

Directions

In a medium-size stockpot, combine all
the ingredients except the peppercorns.
Bring to a boil and then reduce the heat
and simmer for 45 minutes. Add the
peppercorns and continue to simmer
for an additional 10 minutes. Use the
broth immediately for cooking or cool in
an ice bath and refrigerate until needed.

TIP: À la Nage

À la nage is a French phrase that
means "swimming." The idea is to
surround your food with a little
broth. (This would be opposed
to drowning your food!) Court
bouillon is often used to make a
"nage" (a light, brothy sauce) for the
item you cooked in it. After cooking,
remove the fish or shellfish and
simmer to reduce slightly. While
simmering, you can add a handful
of fresh herbs like chervil, tarragon,
chives, or basil for more flavor.
Strain the bouillon through a fine-
mesh strainer and add a little salt
to taste and a few tablespoons (28
to 42 g) butter or a touch of cream.
Serve with your fish or shellfish
in a shallow bowl.

CHAPTER FIVE: RELISHES AND REFRIGERATOR PICKLES

"IN THE LAST ANALYSIS, A PICKLE IS A CUCUMBER WITH EXPERIENCE."

—*Irena Chalmers, American food writer*

Growing up, I can hardly remember sitting down to a meal without a pickle or relish on the table. Whether it was tangy bread and butter pickles, colorful mustard pickles, or corn relish, my dad loved a little something extra.

Although I helped my parents can items from their garden, as an adult I haven't had the space to "put things up" and store them. That's why I started making quick pickles and relishes.

This chapter is a collection of recipes that make just enough, a few cups, the size you might typically purchase from the store. Most recipes take only an hour or so to put together. I just make them as I need them.

CORN RELISH

Fresh sweet corn is the key to success with this relish!
It's a vibrant side dish for summer barbecues.

Yield: One 1-pint (475 g) jar

Ingredients

2 ears fresh sweet corn *(see Note)*

1/4 cup (38 g) small-diced red bell
  pepper *(see page 121)*

1/4 cup (40 g) small-diced sweet onion,
  such as Vidalia or Walla Walla

1/4 teaspoon ground mustard

1/4 teaspoon ground black pepper

1 1/2 teaspoons kosher salt

3/4 teaspoon mustard seeds

3/4 teaspoon turmeric

3/4 teaspoon celery seed

1/2 cup (100 g) sugar

1 cup (235 ml) cider vinegar

Directions

Husk the sweet corn and remove the
silk. Place the corn on a cutting board,
stem-side down. Hold the tip of the corn
steady and, using a sharp knife, slice the
kernels away from the cob. Place the kernels
in a medium-size mixing bowl. Add the
diced red pepper and sweet onion. Stir
to mix. Set aside.

Combine the remaining ingredients in
a medium-size saucepan. Bring to a boil
over high heat. Stir in the mixed vegetables.
Reduce the heat and simmer for 5 minutes
until the corn is tender-crisp.

Spoon the relish out of the brine and
into a sterilized pint (475 ml) jar *(see page 75)*.
Pour the brine over the relish to fill
the jar. You will have extra brine, but
it's the best way to cook the vegetables.
Discard any leftover brine.

Allow to cool to room temperature.
Then cover and refrigerate overnight
before serving. The remaining relish
can be stored, covered, in the refrigerator
for up to 1 month.

Note: If fresh sweet corn is out of season,
you can use 1 1/2 cups (246 g) frozen yellow
corn kernels, thawed.

TRI-COLORED ONION RELISH

This fun colorful relish is really versatile. It's a great accompaniment to hot dogs and sausages, as well as grilled or roasted pork or chicken.

Yield: About 1 cup (245 g)

Ingredients

1/2 cup (120 ml) distilled vinegar

1 tablespoon (12 g) sugar

1/3 cup (53 g) thinly slivered red onion

1/3 cup (53 g) thinly slivered yellow onion

1/3 cup (53 g) thinly slivered sweet onion

1/4 cup (38 g) julienned red bell pepper

1/4 teaspoon red pepper flakes

Directions

Combine the vinegar and sugar in a small saucepan. Warm gently over low heat until the sugar has dissolved.

Add the onions, red bell pepper, and red pepper flakes. Stir to coat and submerge the vegetables. Remove from the heat and let rest for 1 hour.

When the relish is cool, transfer to the refrigerator and chill until the onions are crisp, about 2 hours.

Sliver vs. Slice

Slivers are lateral cuts: think lengthwise. Slices are horizontal cuts: think crosswise. Start by cutting the onion in half lengthwise from the stem (top) to the root (base). This will give you a flat, stable work surface. Turn the onion cut-side down and continue as directed.

Here are some photos to clarify the two cuts. Slivered onions (top) are cut through the onion from root to tip. Sliced onions (bottom) are cut across the onion.

CUCUMBER RELISH

This cucumber relish is the perfect accompaniment for fish, particularly salmon.

You can also use it to make a shrimp salad by combining 1/2 cup (60 g) cucumber relish, 1/2 cup (115 g) mayonnaise, 1 pound (455 g) bay shrimp and/or crab, a little extra minced fresh dill, and a squeeze of lemon juice, if you like.

Yield: About 2 cups (245 g)

Ingredients

2 medium-size cucumbers,
   peeled and seeded

2 tablespoons (18 g) minced
   red bell pepper *(see page 121)*

2 teaspoons grated onion *(see page 18)*

1 tablespoon (4 g) minced fresh dill

1 1/2 teaspoons sea salt or kosher salt

Pinch of freshly ground black pepper

1/4 cup (60 g) mayonnaise *(see page 10)*

4 1/2 teaspoons (23 ml) white wine
   vinegar or rice vinegar

Directions

Mince the peeled and seeded cucumbers *(see sidebar)*. Scoop the minced cucumbers into a clean kitchen towel. Gather the edges together and wring out over the sink until the cucumbers have released most of their liquid.

Place the squeezed cucumbers in a medium-size mixing bowl and stir in the remaining ingredients. Transfer to the refrigerator to chill thoroughly, about 2 hours. Drain off any accumulated liquid before serving. Refrigerate for up to 3 days.

TIP: Cucumber Relish vs. Pickle Relish
When does a cucumber become a pickle? In this case, the difference comes down to whether it is cooked or uncooked. Cucumber relish is lightly marinated, while pickle relish is cooked in a brine.

How to Seed a Cucumber
Removing the seeds from cucumbers can help reduce bitterness and moisture. The easiest way to remove them is to use a teaspoon. First, peel the cucumber and slice it in half lengthwise. Next, use a teaspoon to scoop away the pulp and seeds. Now, you are ready to slice and dice.

SWEET PICKLE RELISH
Bring on the hot dogs!

Yield: One 1-pint (475 ml) jar

Ingredients

1 pound (455 g) pickling cucumbers
  (about 4 or 5), washed and cut
  into large chunks

1/4 red bell pepper, washed and seeded

1 medium-size onion, quartered

4 teaspoons (20 g) kosher salt

1 1/3 cups (315 ml) boiling water

1/4 teaspoon mustard seed

1/8 teaspoon celery seed

3/4 cup (150 g) sugar

1/2 cup (120 ml) distilled white vinegar

Directions

Place the cucumbers, red pepper, and onion into a food processor and pulse until the vegetables are evenly chopped and a fine relish consistency. For a coarser consistency, you can dice the vegetables small by hand.

In a medium-size nonreactive mixing bowl, combine the finely chopped vegetables, salt, and boiling water. Let stand for 1 hour. Drain well before using.

Place the drained vegetables and remaining ingredients in a medium-size, nonreactive saucepan. Bring to a boil over high heat and then lower the heat and simmer, uncovered, until the mixture is thickened and most of the liquid has evaporated, about 20 to 30 minutes. Stir occasionally.

When the relish has finished cooking, transfer it into a sterilized pint (475 ml) jar *(see page 75)*, refrigerate until cool, and then cover. Store in the refrigerator for up to 2 months.

Note: For a true sweet pickle relish consistency, I prefer to chop by hand, but using the food processor definitely saves time.

Ring My Bell

Bell peppers can be quite thick. If you are following a recipe that requires minced or finely chopped bell peppers, you may wish to trim away some of the inner membrane and ribs. Here's how.

Cut the bell pepper in half lengthwise, from stem to base. Use a paring knife to remove the stem and the seeds. Then slice the pepper lengthwise again. If the pepper is very cylindrical, you may need to slice each segment in half again. The idea is to achieve the flattest work surface possible.

Lay the segments flat on your cutting board, skin-side down. Use a chef's knife or paring knife to carefully shave a layer of rib and inner membrane away. Place the blade flat at one edge of the pepper. Hold the edge of the pepper and slice away from your fingertips horizontally. Try to keep the blade level and even. Don't cut too deep or you will leave holes in the skin. Repeat with the remaining segments.

When all the segments are smooth, select one and slice it into long strips, 1/8 inch (3 mm) thick for fine or 1/4 inch (6 mm) thick for small. Group the strips into bundles of 3 to 5. Hold the strips snuggly with your non-cutting hand. Make sure that the ends are lined up evenly. Now, begin to cut the strips horizontally into cubes that are the same thickness as the strips.

You should end up with even cubes. Don't worry if they aren't perfect. Perfect is for fancy French restaurants and molecular gastronomy kitchens. With time and a little practice you'll improve.

Finely chopped bell pepper makes a beautiful garnish. I like to sprinkle red bell pepper on mini tostada bites. They also look pretty sprinkled on salads, fish or chicken breasts, or in clear soups.

CHOW-CHOW

Living in the Pacific Northwest, we usually have a few tomatoes left unripened at the end of the summer. Making chow-chow is a great way to use them up.

Yield: One 1-pint (475 ml) jar

Ingredients

1/2 cup (80g) finely chopped onion

1/2 cup (45 g) finely chopped
green cabbage

1/2 cup (90 g) finely chopped
green tomatoes

1/4 cup (38 g) finely chopped
green bell peppers

1/4 cup (38 g) finely chopped
red bell peppers *(see page 121)*

1 tablespoon (15 g) kosher salt

3/4 cup (150 g) sugar

3/4 teaspoon whole yellow mustard seed

1/8 teaspoon celery seed

1/8 teaspoon turmeric

1/2 cup (120 ml) distilled white vinegar

1/4 cup (60 ml) water

Directions

Combine all the vegetables in a large ceramic or glass mixing bowl. Sprinkle with salt and toss to coat. Cover and let stand overnight.

Transfer the vegetables to a large colander and rinse thoroughly under cold running water. Drain thoroughly.

Mix the sugar, mustard, celery seed, turmeric, vinegar, and water in medium-size saucepan. Add the drained vegetables and stir to combine. Bring the mixture to a boil and then reduce the heat and simmer for 3 to 5 minutes. Spoon into a clean, sterilized pint (475 ml) jar *(see page 75)*. Let cool to room temperature. Then cover and refrigerate until fully chilled, about 2 hours. Store in the refrigerator for up to 3 months.

Note: This is another relish that you can use a food processor to make. The texture is pretty fine.

What the Heck Is Chow-Chow?

Chow-chow, sometimes referred to as piccalilli, is a traditional accompaniment to Southern-style baked beans, black-eyed peas, and greens, but is super on hot dogs, hamburgers, and sandwiches and with cold meats and sausages.

NELL'S MUSTARD PICKLES

This is a variation of my Grandmother Redline's mustard pickle. It's a chunky relish that reminds me a little of Italian giardiniera. You eat it out of the jar, put it on an antipasto platter, or serve it as a side salad.

Yield: Two 1-quart (950 ml) jars

Ingredients

2 cups (200 g) cauliflower florets

1 cup (150 g) 1-inch (2.5 cm) chunks green bell peppers

2 cups (180 g) 1-inch (2.5 cm) chunks green cabbage

1/2 cup (50 g) 1-inch (2.5 cm) chunks celery

1 cup (135 g) 1-inch (2.5 cm) chunks cucumber, peeled or unpeeled

1 medium-size carrot, peeled and cut into 1-inch (2.5 cm) pieces

1 cup (360 g) large-diced green tomatoes

2 cups (340 g) frozen lima beans or (300 g) shelled edamame, thawed

1 1/2 teaspoons coarse kosher salt

4 1/2 teaspoons (16 g) Ballpark-Style Mustard *(see page 22)*

2 cups (475 ml) distilled vinegar

3/4 teaspoon turmeric

1 cup (200 g) sugar

1 tablespoon (8 g) potato starch, cornstarch, or arrowroot powder

Directions

In a large saucepan, combine 3 quarts (2.8 L) water and 2 teaspoons salt. Bring to a boil over high heat. Working in batches, blanch the vegetables until just tender. Do not overcook. Here are a list of estimated blanching times for each vegetable.

Cauliflower—3 minutes
Green peppers—30 seconds
Cabbage—30 seconds
Celery—30 seconds
Cucumber—30 seconds
Carrots—3 minutes
Green tomatoes—30 seconds
Lima beans—Do not blanch. They were blanched when frozen.

I use a blanching basket to make it easier to get the vegetable in and out of the water. As you remove each blanched ingredient from the water, tap the basket lightly over the pot to drain, and then dump the vegetables together in a large mixing bowl. Use a large spoon to gently stir and mix the vegetables. Pour off any water that has accumulated in the bowl and spoon the mixed vegetables into the sterilized quart (950 ml) jars *(see page 75)*.

In a medium-size saucepan, combine the remaining ingredients. Whisk to blend. Bring to a boil over medium-high heat. Reduce the heat and simmer, stirring occasionally, until thickened, about 5 minutes. Pour the sauce over the vegetables.

Allow to cool to room temperature and then cover and refrigerate for at least 2 weeks. The pickles can be stored in the refrigerator for up to 3 months.

BREAD AND BUTTER PICKLES

Bread and butter pickles always remind me of my dad.
He likes to eat them alongside a good sandwich. These are
a lovely accompaniment to ham and Swiss. You can also chop
them up to use in potato salad or macaroni salad.

*Yield: Two 1-pint (475 ml) jars or one
1-quart (950 ml) jar*

Ingredients

6 pickling cucumbers, each 4 to 5 inches
   (10 to 13 cm) long

1/2 large sweet onion

2 tablespoons (30 g) kosher salt

4 cups (945 ml) water

1 cup (235 ml) distilled white vinegar

1/2 cup (115 g) packed light brown sugar

1/2 teaspoon celery seed

1/2 teaspoon turmeric

1/2 teaspoon mustard seeds

Directions

Wash and slice the cucumbers into thin
slices, about 1/8 inch (3 mm) thick. This
is best accomplished using a mandoline,
if you have one *(see page 143)*. Place in a large
glass or ceramic mixing bowl.

Slice the onion in half from stem to root.
Slice off the stem end of the onion. Leaving
the root intact, peel away the skin of the
onion. Place the peeled onion cut-side
down on a cutting board and, starting
at the stem end, slice into 1/4-inch (6 mm)
slices. Add the onion to the cucumbers.

In a separate bowl, combine the kosher salt
and water. Stir until the salt has dissolved.
Pour over the cucumbers and onion
and allow to brine at room temperature
for 2 hours.

Drain the cucumbers and onion in
a colander and rinse thoroughly with
cool water. Drain.

Combine the vinegar, brown sugar,
celery seed, turmeric, and mustard seeds
in a medium-size saucepan. Bring to
a boil over high heat. Add the cucumbers
and onion. Reduce the heat and simmer
for 10 minutes. Remove from the heat
and allow to cool to room temperature.
Transfer the pickles to a sterilized jar
(see page 75). Cover and refrigerate for up
to 3 months.

Not Your Average Sweet Pickle

There isn't a definitive answer for how bread and butter pickles got their name, but here are a couple origin stories I found:

Number one—Bread and butter pickles got their name during the Depression when they were as common as bread and butter during a meal.

Number two—Bread and butter pickles got their name from the common Victorian practice of serving bread and butter with pickles.

I am voting for number two, myself, but your guess is as good as mine.

Even if you are not a big fan of sweet pickles, you might find that you enjoy bread and butter pickles. There's a savory component to them with the addition of onion, mustard seed, and celery seed. Give 'em a shot! Trust me.

MRS. ROLLER'S GARLIC-DILL REFRIGERATOR PICKLES

Bonnie Roller was a girlhood friend of my mother. Mom used to tell a story about Bonnie standing on the picnic table in her front yard held hostage by geese while waiting for the school bus. When the bus pulled up, Bonnie would leap from the picnic table with the geese in hot pursuit. I never met Bonnie, but I've eaten her mother's pickles. I can't eat these pickles without smiling about a girl and some geese.

Yield: Four 1-pint (475 ml) jars

Ingredients

2 pounds (910 g) pickling cucumbers

4 cloves garlic, peeled (1 clove per jar)

1 jalapeño pepper, seeded and cut
    into lengthwise strips

8 sprigs fresh dill (2 sprigs per jar)

12 peppercorns (3 peppercorns per jar)

4 grape leaves, canned or fresh
    (1 leaf per jar) *(see Note)*

1 cup (235 ml) distilled white vinegar

3 cups (700 ml) water

1/4 cup (60 g) kosher salt

Directions

Place the cucumbers in a large bowl. Cover with cold water and refrigerate for 24 hours to crisp.

When the cucumbers are done soaking, wash and quarter them lengthwise or leave whole. Whole cucumbers take longer for the flavor to pickle, but if you don't mind the wait, you can pack them uncut. If you choose to leave the pickles whole you may want to pack them into two 1-quart jars (950 ml) instead of four 1-pint (475 ml) jars.

Heat about 2 cups (475 ml) water in a small saucepan over high heat. When the water comes to a boil, drop in the garlic cloves and blanch for 30 seconds. Remove the cloves from the boiling water and rinse under cold water until cool.

Arrange the sterilized jars *(see page 75)* on the counter and fill each jar with 1 garlic clove, 1 or 2 jalapeño strips, 2 sprigs of dill, and 3 peppercorns. (Double the amount of spices per jar if using quart jars instead of pints.) Pack the cucumbers firmly into the jars. You don't want to damage them, but you do want them packed tight.

If you are using fresh grape leaves, fill a small saucepan with water. Bring the water to a boil. Drop in the fresh grape leaves and blanch for 30 seconds. Carefully remove the leaves using tongs or a slotted spoon. Pat dry on a clean towel and set aside.

If you are using canned grape leaves, place a bundle of leaves in a bowl of cold water for 5 minutes. Then, carefully unroll the bundle to separate the leaves. Pat the leaves dry with a clean towel and set aside.

In a medium-size saucepan, combine the vinegar, water, and salt. Bring to a boil. Pour the brine into the jars, leaving about 1/2 inch (1.3 cm) of space from the top of the rim.

Tap the jars gently on the countertop to dislodge any trapped air bubbles. Remember, the brine is hot, so take care not to burn yourself. Lay a single grape leaf on top of the pickles in each jar.

Apply the lids and let the jars cool to room temperature. When the jars have cooled, place them in the refrigerator. Ideally, they should pickle for at least 6 weeks for optimum flavor, but I know it's hard to wait. So, try to let them sit for at least 1 week before eating. If you are making whole pickles, let them sit for at least 3 weeks before eating.

Note: Grape leaves contain tannins that hamper the enzymes that make pickles soft. However, if you remove the blossom ends of the cucumbers (the source of undesirable enzymes), the addition of grape leaves may be unnecessary. I add them because I've had success making the pickles with them and they grow nearby. Other tannin-rich leaves that you might substitute include raspberry and horseradish.

Mrs. Roller's original recipe called for alum, a salt compound, which is a bit controversial in pickling these days. Alum was used to improve firmness and ensure crisp pickles. You can add it to the initial cold water soak of the cucumbers, if you wish—1/2 teaspoon is plenty.

PICKLED ONIONS

Whether you enjoy a Gibson Martini or a Bloody Mary, or just want a delicious addition to your relish trays or antipasto platters, these perky little onions are perfect.

Yield: One 1-pint (475 ml) jar

Ingredients

1 tablespoon (15 g) salt

1 cup (235 ml) water

2 cups (300 g) frozen pearl onions, thawed, or fresh spring onions

1 cup (235 ml) cider vinegar

1 tablespoon (6 g) pickling spice

1 bay leaf

Directions

If using fresh spring onions, peel and trim them. Next, bring a medium-sized saucepan of water to a boil, add the onions, and blanch them for 3 to 5 minutes, depending on their size. Remove from the saucepan. Drain the onions through a colander and immediately submerge them in the ice bath to refresh them. When the onions have cooled completely, drain and follow the directions below for brining.

In a small mixing bowl, create a brine solution by dissolving the salt in cool water. Stir until the salt completely disappears.

Place the onions in the brine. Make sure that they are completely submerged. You may need to place a small saucer on top to weight them down. Refrigerate for 24 hours.

The next day, combine the vinegar, pickling spice, and bay leaf in a small nonreactive saucepan. Warm over medium heat. When the vinegar is just about to boil, remove the pan from the heat and allow the mixture to cool for 2 hours. This will infuse the flavors. After 2 hours, strain out the spices.

Drain the onions and rinse them under cool water. Pack the onions tightly into a sterilized 1-pint (475 ml) jar *(see page 75)*. If any water leaks out of the onions, pour it off before adding the spiced vinegar. Cover the jar and refrigerate for at least 3 weeks. The longer you wait, the more pickled and intense the flavor will become. The pickled onions can be used for up to 6 months, if stored in the refrigerator.

SPICY PICKLED CARROTS

I love the hint of spice in these carrots. You can make them mild or hot by adjusting the amount of jalapeños you add.

Yield: One 1-quart (950 ml) jar

Ingredients

2 or 3 medium-size jalapeño peppers *(see Note)*

4 cups (950 ml) water

1 teaspoon kosher salt

3 cups (390 g) peeled and ¼-inch (6 mm) bias-sliced carrots *(see sidebar)*

1 cup (160 g) slivered sweet onion

1 clove garlic, peeled

2 cups (475 ml) distilled white vinegar

1 tablespoon (12 g) sugar

1 tablespoon (15 g) kosher salt

1 large bay leaf

Directions

Slice the jalapeño peppers in half lengthwise. Remove the stems and seeds. Or, for a spicier version, leave the peppers whole and slice them crosswise into ¼-inch (6 mm) rings instead.

Fill a medium saucepan with the water and salt. Bring to a boil. Meanwhile, fill a large mixing bowl with 2 quarts (1.9 L) water and 4 cups (1 kg) ice to make an ice bath.

When the water is boiling, plunge the carrot slices into the water and blanch for 2 to 3 minutes. Drain the carrots through a colander and then immediately submerge them in the ice bath to refresh them.

Place the jalapeños, carrots, onion, and garlic in sterilized 1-quart (950 ml) jar *(see page 75)*. Layer the vegetables to mix the flavors and to make them look attractive.

Add the vinegar, sugar, kosher salt, and bay leaf to a large nonreactive saucepan and bring to a boil. Pour the hot vinegar into the jar on top of the layered vegetables. As you are filling, tap the jar slightly on the counter to release any pockets of air between the vegetables. You should have enough vinegar to completely cover the vegetables, but don't overfill the jar. Leave about ½ inch (1.3 cm) of space from the top of the rim.

Let the mixture cool to room temperature and then transfer the uncovered jar to the refrigerator. When the mixture is fully chilled, cover with a lid.

Store, covered, in the refrigerator for up to 2 months. Remember, the spiciness will increase over time!

Note: When working with chiles and hot peppers, it's a good idea to wear disposable latex gloves to protect your skin. Or if your bare hands are exposed, wash them with a mild bleach solution (1 part bleach to 3 parts water) to remove the oils; dip your hands into the solution briefly and then dry them with a paper towel.

How to Make Bias Cuts

Sounds more like a dressmaking term than a culinary one, doesn't it? A bias cut, also called a diagonal cut, is most commonly used in stir-frying. That's actually a good idea to keep in mind when you are making bias cuts because stir-fried vegetables are cut thin to cook quickly and a good bias cut is usually about 1/4 inch (6 mm) thick or so.

Carrots are a bit tricky to cut on the bias because they are round and keeping them steady can be an issue. You can either leave them whole or split them lengthwise to give yourself a flat, stable base.

PICKLED PEPPERS

These peppers are a wonderful addition
to a picnic basket. Serve alongside cold fried
or roasted chicken.

Yield: Two 1-pint (475 ml) jars

Ingredients

1 large green bell pepper

1 large red bell pepper

1/2 cup (80 g) slivered white onion

1 1/4 cups (295 ml) distilled white vinegar

1 cup (200 g) sugar

2 1/2 teaspoons dried tarragon

3 1/2 teaspoons (18 g) kosher salt

Directions

Wash the bell peppers thoroughly. Slice
each pepper in half and remove the
seeds and ribs (white portions). Slice the
peppers into thin strips. Pack he peppers
and onions snuggly into sterilized pint
(475 ml) jars *(see page 75)*.

Meanwhile, in a small nonreactive saucepan,
combine the vinegar, sugar, tarragon,
and salt. Bring to a boil. Reduce the heat
and simmer until the sugar and salt have
dissolved, about 5 minutes. Pour the hot
vinegar over the peppers. Allow to sit
at room temperature until cool and then
cover and refrigerate for 1 week. You can
certainly eat some of the peppers before
the week is up, but the flavor will intensify
with time. The peppers can be refrigerated
for up to 1 month.

Tarragon

Tarragon is such an underutilized herb. Perhaps it's because people have an aversion to licorice, but to simply equate tarragon with licorice is a disservice. The herb is so much more refined and delicate than that.

French tarragon is considered the best for cooking. As a matter of fact, it is part of the classic French fines herbes blend—chervil, parsley, thyme, and tarragon—which are fabulous in simple omelets and salads or as a coating for soft goat cheeses.

Here are a few other ways I love to use tarragon:

• Tarragon is at the core of béarnaise sauce. Rich, eggy, and herbaceous it makes my mouth water for a filet just thinking about it

• Add to mayonnaise *(see page 10)*, then use for chicken or shrimp salad.

• Use a little dried tarragon sprinkled in eggs before lightly scrambling them. Spoon those tarragon scrambled eggs over spears of buttered asparagus ... oh my.

• Sprinkle a teaspoon or so of minced fresh tarragon on top of glazed carrots.

• Steep sprigs in wine vinegar for a classic French vinegar *(see page 74)*.

• Combine 1 tablespoon (4 g) fresh tarragon with 2 tablespoons (28 g) soft butter. Smear it on a whole chicken. Season with salt and pepper and roast as usual.

• Make a tarragon butter sauce (beurre blanc) for mild white fish or scallops.

PICKLED GREEN BEANS

Crunchy with a hint of garlic, these green beans are totally addictive.

Yield: One 1-pint (475 ml) jar

Ingredients

6 to 8 ounces (170 to 225 g) fresh green
   beans, as straight as you can find

1 clove garlic, peeled

1 small dried chile *(optional)*

1 bay leaf

1/8 teaspoon dill seeds or pinch
   of dried dillweed

3 or 4 whole black peppercorns

3/4 cup (180 ml) distilled vinegar

1/4 cup (60 ml) water

1 tablespoon (12 g) sugar

1 1/4 teaspoons kosher salt

Directions

Wash the green beans and, if necessary, trim the ends so the beans will fit standing up in the pint jar.

Heat about 1 cup (235 ml) water in a small saucepan over high heat. When the water comes to a boil, drop in the garlic clove and blanch for 30 seconds. Drain the clove and rinse under cold water until cool.

Pack the green beans into a sterilized pint (475 ml) jar *(see page 75)*. Tuck the garlic clove, chile, bay leaf, dill, and peppercorns among the beans.

In the meantime, combine the vinegar, water, sugar, and salt in a small nonreactive saucepan. Bring to a boil over high heat. When the sugar and salt have dissolved, pour the hot liquid into the jar over the beans. Cover the jar and allow it to cool to room temperature. Refrigerate for at least 1 week to allow the flavors to infuse. Store for up to 3 months in the refrigerator.

TIP: Got the Blues?

If you notice a bluish tinge to your garlic cloves, don't worry. Compounds in garlic sometimes react with the acidity of the vinegar, creating a bluing effect, particularly if the pickling process is slower, as with that of refrigerator pickles. Blanching the garlic seems to help but doesn't guarantee the garlic will remain white. In any case, the blue garlic is perfectly safe to eat.

SAUERKRAUT

I owe a special thanks to Julie O'Brien and Richard Climenhage,
of Firefly Kitchens, for all their expert advice and suggestions.

Yield: One 1-quart (950 ml) jar

Ingredients

2 1/2 pounds (1.1 kg) green cabbage,
  shredded or chopped

1 1/2 to 2 tablespoons (23 to 30 g) sea salt

1 teaspoon caraway seeds, dill seeds, juniper
  berries, or whole coriander *(optional)*

Directions

Sterilize a quart (950 ml) jar *(see page 75)*.
Fill it with water and close.

In large mixing bowl, mix the cabbage
thoroughly with the salt using your
hands or tongs. If using your hands,
make sure that they are very clean prior
to mixing. Let stand for 10 minutes.
Mix in the spice.

Pack the cabbage mixture down into
a large plastic food container or crock
(approximately 3 quarts [2.8 L]). Top
with a sterilized plate (one that has been
boiled for 10 minutes) or lid smaller than
the opening of the container and place the
sterilized quart jar filled with water on top of
the plate. Place the container on the counter
overnight. Room temperature, between 65º
and 70ºF (18º and 21ºC), is best to get
the process started.

In about 24 hours, the cabbage should have
given up enough juice to be completely
submerged. If there isn't sufficient juice

brine to cover the cabbage after 24
hours, add more brine. Simply dissolve
2 teaspoons sea salt in 1 cup (235 ml)
water and pour it over the cabbage.

Find a spot on the counter or in your pantry
to store the container. Check the container
every other day to make sure the kraut
stays submerged completely in brine.

While the kraut is fermenting, you may
notice white film growing on the surface.
Don't be afraid. This can happen due to
yeast in the air. However, if your sauerkraut
develops blackish or greenish mold,
becomes slimy or discolored (pink or
brownish), or smells funky (not in a
sauerkraut way), discard it.

Allow the sauerkraut to ferment at room
temperature for at least 2 weeks; however,
4 to 6 weeks would be better. Longer
fermentation improves the flavor and
ensures that all stages of the fermentation
process are complete.

When the sauerkraut is finished fermenting,
skim away the yeast layer and transfer the
kraut and its juices to a sterilized jar. Store
in the refrigerator for up to 3 months.

Note: I've seen people use a zip-top
bag filled with brine solution as a weight
instead of a jar of water. There are also
special crocks that come with ceramic
weights for fermentation.

CHAPTER SIX: CHIPS, DIPS, AND DUNKS

"POTATO CHIPS, POTATO CHIPS, I LOVE POTATO CHIPS. POTATO CHIPS, POTATO CHIPS, EAT 'EM UP, WOW."

—*Radio jingle, The Ben Stiller Show*

Chips and dips are my weakness. I love them—perhaps a little too much. I might pass up a good piece of chocolate for a thick, crunchy chip with a savory dip. Well okay, I might struggle over the decision for a second or two. Anyway, this chapter contains a darn good selection of chips and dips from potato to pita and sour cream to salsa. If you are anything like me, you'll have to pace yourself. No more than two or three dip recipes a day!

HOMEMADE POTATO CHIPS

Even slices are the key to consistent chips,
so unless you've got an eagle eye and a steady hand,
using a mandoline is your best bet.

Yield: 4 to 8 servings

Ingredients

1 pound (455 g) russet or Idaho potatoes,
    peeled or simply scrubbed clean

About 8 cups (1.9 L) rice bran oil,
    canola oil, or beef tallow, for frying

Fine sea salt, to taste

Directions

Slice the potatoes very thinly, 1/8 inch
(3 mm) or thinner. Place the slices in a bowl
of cold water. Add a handful of ice cubes
to help crisp the slices. Allow to chill
for 30 minutes.

In a deep fryer or heavy-bottomed
stockpot, heat the oil to 320º to 350ºF
(160º to 180ºC).

Line a cookie sheet with paper towels.

Pour the sliced potatoes through a colander
to drain. Remove any unmelted ice cubes
and pat the potatoes dry with a clean
kitchen towel or paper towels.

Using a blanching basket, stir-fry spider,
or slotted spoon, fry batches of potatoes
until golden and crisp on both sides, about
5 to 7 minutes. Stirring the potatoes gently
as you fry can help them crisp evenly and
not clump together. Drain the potatoes
of excess oil over the fryer, transfer them
to the prepared cookie sheet, and season
with salt.

Cool to room temperature before serving.
Store any uneaten potato chips (yeah, like
that's gonna happen) in an airtight container
at room temperature for up to 1 day.

Variation: **Truffled Potato Chips**—Season
with truffle salt and instead of regular
sea salt for a pungent, garlicky burst.
Add a sprinkle of minced fresh parsley
(see page 14) for color.

Truffle Salt

Truffles are one of the most prized and expensive ingredients in the gourmet world. A truffle is a fungus (think woody subterranean tuber) that grows underground or beneath the leafy detritus at the roots of oak, chestnut, hazel, and beech trees. You've probably seen the quintessential image of a pig at the end of a leash, routing in the dirt to nose out a truffle, followed closely by an old man in a beret. Pigs used to be the primary beast for finding truffles, but they're quite fond of the fungi and could easily eat up the profits before the forager could get a hand on them. Over the past couple of decades more dogs have been trained to search for the pricey nuggets.

The flavor of a truffle can be quite pungent—imagine if a head of garlic and a woodsy mushroom had a baby. The two most common types are black and white. Popular in Western Europe, they are used to flavor beef dishes, risottos, eggs, cheeses, and pastas. A little goes a long way, particularly with the stronger flavored black truffles; they are usually shaved paper-thin or grated for cooking or finishing a dish.

Truffle salt is a fun and flavorful way to get a sense of truffles without breaking the bank. It is typically a combination of sea salt and tiny flakes or specks of truffle—earthy, garlicky, salty. I love to sprinkle it on french fries and potato chips, as I mentioned, and buttered popcorn. You can use truffle salt in much the same way you'd us a fresh truffle, so experiment by adding a dash to risotto, scramble eggs, or mashed potatoes. It's also wonderful on radishes. Or rub some on a steak before you cook it.

SWEET POTATO CHIPS

Sweet potatoes are higher in natural sugar
than are other tubers, so you'll need to cook them
in cooler oil than that used for regular potato chips.

Yield: 4 to 8 servings

Ingredients

2 large sweet potatoes or yams, peeled
    or simply scrubbed clean

About 8 cups (1.9 L) rice bran oil
    or canola oil, for frying

Fine sea salt, to taste

Directions

Using a mandoline, slice the sweet potatoes very thinly, about 1/8 inch (3 mm).

Place the slices into a bowl of cold water. Add a few ice cubes. The cold water helps crisp the chips before frying.

In a deep fryer or heavy-bottomed stockpot, heat the oil to 300°F (150°C). Try to maintain the temperature between 300°F (150°C) and no more than 325°F (170°C). You can use a candy thermometer to monitor the temperature of the oil. Remember, the higher concentration of sugar in sweet potatoes has a tendency to scorch at higher temperatures, so watch your heat.

Line a cookie sheet with paper towels.

Drain the sweet potato slices and pat them dry, gently. Working in batches, fry the sweet potatoes until crispy on both sides, about 4 to 5 minutes. I use a stir-fry spider or slotted spoon to carefully stir the potatoes while frying. Drain the potatoes of excess oil over the fryer, transfer them to the prepared cookie sheet, and season with salt.

Cool to room temperature before serving. Unfortunately, sweet potato chips can get limp if you try to store them too long, so you'll have to eat them all the first day.

Variation: **Cinnamon Sugar Sweet Potato Chips**—Season with cinnamon sugar instead of salt for a special treat. Combine 1/4 cup (50 g) sugar with 1 teaspoon cinnamon in a small bowl. Transfer to a shaker or fine-mesh strainer and sprinkle over the freshly fried chips.

How to Use a Mandoline

Mandolines are handy to use if you are a fan of sautéed, grilled, or fried vegetables. They are the easiest way to get even slices fast. Why would you care if your slices are even? Imagine a slab of zucchini on a grill, the paper-thin end scorching and burning, while the thick end is taking forever to cook. Even thickness equals even cooking.

To properly use a mandoline, adjust the blade to the desired thickness. Place the item you will be slicing on the ramp above the blade. If the item is very tall or

long, such as a sweet potato or zucchini, you can hold it with your hand for the first few slices. However, you must be very careful not to cut yourself. Most mandolines come with a pusher or guard to protect your fingers.

Slide the item toward the blade. Don't press down too hard or you may find that the vegetable builds up suction and won't slide easily. Concentrate on pushing away gently toward the blade.

ROOT VEGETABLE CHIPS

This blend is typical of some commercial brands.
However, you should feel free to substitute other vegetables.
You could include purple potatoes, Chioggia beets,
golden beets, or parsnips.

Yield: 4 to 8 servings

Ingredients

1 pound (455 g) taro roots,
   washed and peeled

1 pound (455 g) sweet potatoes,
   washed and peeled, if desired

1 pound (455 g) yams, washed
   and peeled, if desired

1 pound (455 g) red beets, washed
   and peeled

About 8 cups (1.9 L) rice bran oil,
   canola oil, or grapeseed oil, for frying

Fine sea salt, to taste

Directions

Slice the vegetables very thinly, 1/8 inch (3 mm) or thinner. Group the vegetables by type into separate bowls of cold water. Add a handful of ice cubes to help crisp the slices. Allow to chill for 30 minutes.

In a deep fryer or heavy-bottomed stockpot, heat the oil to 300ºF (150ºC). Try to maintain the temperature between 300ºF (150ºC) and no more than 325ºF (170ºC) so the chips don't scorch.

Prepare 2 baking sheet by lining them with multiple layers of paper towels or brown paper shopping bags for draining the chips.

Working in batches, drain and pat each group of vegetables dry using paper towels to avoid staining, particularly from the beets.

Starting with the taro, fry the vegetables in batches until lightly golden and crisp, about 5 to 7 minutes per batch. (Cooking time varies with oil temperature and thickness of chips.) Stir the vegetables gently using a long slotted spoon or stir-fry spider to ensure even browning. When the chips are crisp, remove them from the fryer, allowing excess oil to drain away before placing the chips on the paper towels. Salt the hot chips immediately and start the next batch of vegetables. I suggest frying the beets last because they can stain the oil slightly and make all the chips a little rosy.

When you've fried all the chips, allow them to cool to room temperature and then toss them together in a large bowl and serve.

Note: The skin on the sweet potatoes and yams is fairly thin, so peeling them is optional. It's your choice.

FRENCH ONION DIP

My friend Cathy says this dip is right out of the *Mad Men* era.
I say pass the Bugles!

Yield: 2 1/2 cups (575 g)

Ingredients

1 tablespoon (15 ml) canola oil
  or rice bran oil

1 tablespoon (14 g) butter

2 cups (320 g) small-diced onion

1 tablespoon (15 ml) brandy

2 cups (460 g) sour cream

1/4 teaspoon celery salt

1 teaspoon Worcestershire sauce *(see page 36)*

1 teaspoon grated onion *(see page 18)*
      or 1/4 teaspoon onion powder

3/4 teaspoon coarse sea salt or kosher salt

1/4 teaspoon ground white pepper

1/4 teaspoon garlic powder

Pinch of thyme

Directions

Warm the oil and butter in a medium-size sauté pan over medium heat. When the butter is melted, add the onion and cook, stirring occasionally, until golden brown and caramelized, about 20 to 30 minutes. Add the brandy to the pan and stir, scraping any browned bits of onion from the bottom of the pan. Simmer until the brandy is completely evaporated, about 30 seconds to 1 minute. Remove the onions from the heat and allow them to cool to room temperature.

Meanwhile, in a medium bowl, combine the sour cream, celery salt, Worcestershire sauce, grated onion, salt, pepper, garlic powder, and thyme. Stir in the cooled onions. Chill for at least 1 hour or overnight before serving.

SCALLION DIP

This is my favorite go-to dip. It takes no time at all
to make and is yummy. Yay!

Yield: 2 1/4 cups (518 g)

Ingredients

2 cups (460 g) sour cream

1/2 cup (50 g) sliced scallions

2 tablespoons (8 g) minced
   fresh parsley *(see page 14)*

1 teaspoon Dijon mustard *(see page 29)*

1 teaspoon white wine vinegar

1/2 teaspoon garlic purée *(see page 17)*
   or 1/8 teaspoon garlic powder

3/4 teaspoon sea salt or kosher salt

Freshly ground black pepper
   to taste *(optional)*

Directions

Combine all the ingredients in a medium-size mixing bowl. Stir until smooth and fully blended.

Transfer to a serving bowl. Cover with plastic wrap and refrigerate until chilled, at least 1 hour. Taste for additional salt, if desired.

Variation: **Creamy Scallion Dip**—Omit 1/2 cup (115 g) of the sour cream and add 1/2 cup (115 g) mayonnaise *(see page 10)* in its place (i.e., 1 1/2 cups [345 g] sour cream and 1/2 cup [115 g] mayonnaise). Chill thoroughly and serve.

HERB DIP

Whether you are serving fresh vegetables or chips, this dip is delectable with them.

Yield: About 1 1/4 cups (288 g)

Ingredients

1 tablespoon (3 g) minced chives

1/4 teaspoon garlic purée *(see page 17)* or pinch of garlic powder

1 tablespoon (4 g) minced tarragon

2 1/2 teaspoons minced arugula

1 teaspoon freshly squeezed lemon juice

1 cup (230 g) sour cream

1/2 teaspoon coarse sea salt or kosher salt

1/4 teaspoon freshly ground black pepper

Directions

Combine all the ingredients in a small mixing bowl. Stir until thoroughly blended. Cover the bowl and transfer to the refrigerator. Chill for at least 1 hour prior to serving. Store in the refrigerator for up to 5 days.

BLUE CHEESE DIP

This dip is chunky and delicious. It's the perfect combination with a thick, homemade potato chip.

Yield: About 1 3/4 cups (400 g)

Ingredients

4 ounces (115 g) cream cheese,
   at room temperature

3/4 cup (173 g) sour cream

3/4 cup (90 g) blue cheese crumbles

2 tablespoons (12 g) minced scallions

1/4 teaspoon grated onion *(see page 18)*
   or 3/4 teaspoon onion powder

1/2 teaspoon freshly ground black pepper

Dash of Worcestershire sauce *(see page 36)*

Directions

Using a hand mixer or stand mixer, beat the cream cheese on medium speed until soft and creamy, about 2 minutes. Scrape down the sides of the bowl as needed.

Add the sour cream and beat at low speed until combined, about 1 minute. Add the blue cheese crumbles and continue beating until any large lumps are broken up. Stir in the scallions, grated onion, pepper, and Worcestershire sauce.

Transfer the dip to a small serving bowl, cover with plastic wrap, and refrigerate for at least 1 hour or up to 5 days. Serve with potato chips *(see page 140)*, Buffalo wings, or vegetables.

CLAM DIP

Growing up, we always had a party on Christmas Eve.
It was nothing fancy, just a variety of appetizers and chips and dip.
My mother had a 1960s green glass chip bowl with a rack suspending
the dip bowl on one side. We always filled it with clam dip (and
Ruffles). I thought it was the height of sophistication!

Yield: 1 1/4 cups (288 g)

Ingredients

1 cup (230 g) sour cream

1 or 2 cans (6 1/2 ounces, or 182 g each)
   minced clams, drained, 2 tablespoons
   (28 ml) liquid reserved

1 tablespoon (10 g) minced shallot or onion

1 tablespoon (4 g) minced
   fresh parsley *(see page 14)*

1/4 teaspoon Worcestershire sauce *(see page 36)*

1 teaspoon freshly squeezed lemon juice

1/8 teaspoon garlic powder

1/2 teaspoon coarse sea salt or kosher salt

Freshly ground black pepper to taste

1/2 to 1 teaspoon prepared
horseradish *(see page 38)*

Directions

In a small mixing bowl, combine the sour cream, drained clams, shallot, parsley, Worcestershire, lemon juice, garlic powder, salt, pepper, and reserved clam liquid. Stir to blend. Transfer to a serving bowl, cover with plastic wrap, and chill for at least 1 hour prior to serving.

Just before serving, stir in the horseradish. Check the seasoning and add a little more salt or pepper if desired.

This dip is far better when served the same day it is made, so I don't recommend making it in advance. If you need to prepare it the day before, don't add the clams, clam juice, and horseradish until an hour before you plan to serve it. Otherwise, the clams can get a little chewy, and the dip loses its oomph.

PITA CHIPS

The key to crispy pita chips is low and slow.
Toasting too hot will cause your pita chips to burn
before they get completely crunchy.

Yield: 60 pita chips or 8 to 12 servings

Ingredients

5 pieces pocket pita bread, white or wheat

1/2 cup (120 ml) olive oil

Sea salt, to taste

Directions

Preheat the oven to 300ºF (150ºC,
or gas mark 2).

Cut each pita pocket in half and then
stack the halves on top of one another.
Cut the stack into thirds. You will you
have 6 wedges per slice. Then carefully
peel each wedge in half, opening what
was the pocket. Repeat with the remaining
rounds. You will have 60 wedges when
you are done.

Lay the wedges on a large baking sheet.
Using a pastry brush or basting brush,
brush both sides of each wedge with
olive oil. Sprinkle the top of the chips
with sea salt.

Place the baking sheet in the oven and bake
for 25 to 30 minutes until the chips are
golden and crisp. Remove from the oven
and let cool on a wire rack for 15 minutes.

Cooled pita chips can be eaten immediately
or stored in an airtight container for up
to 1 week. They may soften with time. If
so, rewarm them on a baking sheet in a
preheated 350ºF (180ºC, or gas mark 4)
oven for 3 to 5 minutes.

Variations: **Cheesy Garlic Pita Chips—**
Combine 1/2 cup (50 g) grated Parmigiano-
Reggiano cheese with 1/2 teaspoon dried
parsley and 1/4 teaspoon garlic powder
in a small mixing bowl. Sprinkle the pita
chips with the cheese blend during the
last 10 to 15 minutes of baking.

Cinnamon Sugar Pita Chips—Omit the
olive oil and brush the pita chips with
canola oil or melted butter. Combine 1/4 cup
(50 g) sugar with 1 teaspoon cinnamon
and a pinch of nutmeg in a small bowl.
Sprinkle the wedges with the cinnamon
sugar and bake as directed. Serve with
Greek yogurt drizzled with honey.

ARTICHOKE DIP

Gooey, warm, tangy ... this is perfect with pita or tortilla chips.

Yield: About 2 cups (460 g)

Ingredients

2 packages (8 ounces, or 225 g each) cream cheese, at room temperature

½ cup (115 g) mayonnaise *(see page 10)*

2 teaspoons freshly squeezed lemon juice

1 teaspoon Dijon mustard *(see page 29)*

¼ teaspoon original Tabasco sauce *(optional)*

½ teaspoon coarse sea salt or kosher salt

½ teaspoon garlic purée *(see page 17)* or ⅛ teaspoon garlic powder

¼ cup (25 g) sliced scallions

1 package (8 ounces, or 225 g) frozen artichoke hearts, thawed and coarsely chopped

½ cup (40 g) shredded Parmigiano-Reggiano or Asiago cheese, divided

Directions

Preheat the oven to 350ºF (180ºC, or gas mark 4).

Using a hand mixer or stand mixer, beat the cream cheese until smooth and creamy. Add the mayonnaise, lemon juice, mustard, Tabasco, salt, and garlic and continue beating until fully blended, about 2 minutes.

Using a rubber scraper or spoon, fold in the scallions, artichoke hearts, and ¼ cup (20 g) of the Parmigiano-Reggiano. When the ingredients have been incorporated, scrape the dip into a small casserole dish or medium-size cast-iron skillet. Cover the dish with aluminum foil or a tight-fitting lid and bake for 25 minutes until warm and bubbly.

Remove the dish from the oven, uncover, and sprinkle the dip with the remaining ¼ cup (20 g) Parmigiano-Reggiano. Preheat the broiler. Return the dish to the oven and place 4 to 6 inches (10 to 15 cm) from the broiler. Broil until the cheese melts and turns light golden brown, 1 to 2 minutes.

Remove from the oven. Allow to cool slightly, 5 to 10 minutes, and serve. This dip is equally good with tortilla chips *(see page 162)* or pita chips *(see page 152)*.

Store any unused dip in the refrigerator, covered, for up to 5 days. To serve again, cover the dish snuggly in aluminum foil and warm in a 300ºF (150ºC, or gas mark 2) oven for 15 to 20 minutes.

SPINACH DIP

This is a perennial favorite. Who knew you could make it without a packet of soup mix?

Yield: 4 cups (920 g)

Ingredients

¼ cup (60 ml) water

1 package (10 ounces, or 280 g) frozen, chopped spinach, thawed

2 tablespoons (19 g) minced red bell pepper *(see page 121)*

2 tablespoons (16 g) minced carrot

1 cup (225 g) mayonnaise *(see page 10)*

1 ½ cups (345 g) sour cream

1 tablespoon (10 g) grated onion *(see page 18)* or ¼ teaspoon onion powder

2 teaspoons minced fresh parsley *(see page 14)* or 1 teaspoon dried parsley

1 teaspoon coarse sea salt or kosher salt

1 teaspoon freshly squeezed lemon juice

½ teaspoon sugar

¼ teaspoon celery salt

¼ teaspoon sweet paprika

¼ teaspoon freshly ground black pepper

¼ teaspoon garlic powder

1 can (8 ounces, or 225 g) water chestnuts, drained and chopped *(optional)*

Directions

Add the water to a medium-size saucepan. Bring to a boil over high heat. Add the spinach to the pan, cover, and reduce the heat to medium. Cook for 5 minutes, and then stir in the bell pepper and carrot. Cover again and cook for an additional minute.

Remove from the stove top and drain the vegetables through a fine-mesh colander. Rinse immediately with cold water. When the vegetables have cooled, press them firmly with your hand or a large spoon to remove as much excess water as possible. Set aside.

In a medium-size mixing bowl, combine the mayonnaise, sour cream, onion, parsley, salt, lemon juice, sugar, celery salt, paprika, pepper, and garlic. Stir until fully combined. Add the cooled vegetables and the water chestnuts and mix well.

Transfer the dip to the refrigerator and chill for at least 1 hour or overnight. Serve with tortilla chips *(see page 162)* or pita chips *(see page 152)*. Store unused dip, covered, in the refrigerator for up to 5 days.

HUMMUS

I don't even consider buying premade hummus anymore.
This is so much better than the packaged brands.

Yield: About 3 cups (740 g)

Ingredients

1 cup (200 g) dried chickpeas *(see Note)*

1/4 teaspoon baking soda

1 bay leaf

1 teaspoon coarse sea salt or kosher salt,
    plus more to taste

2 cloves garlic

3 tablespoons (45 ml) freshly
    squeezed lemon juice

1/4 cup (60 g) tahini *(see page 53)*

2 tablespoons (28 ml) extra-virgin
    olive oil, plus more for drizzling

Minced fresh parsley *(see page 14)* *(optional)*

Directions

Place the chickpeas in a large glass or
ceramic bowl. Cover with water, stir in
the baking soda, and let sit overnight.
Drain the water the next morning.

Place the beans in a large saucepan.
Cover with fresh water. Add the bay leaf.
Bring to a boil over high heat and then
lower the heat and simmer for 1 1/2 to 2
hours or until the beans are tender. Add
the salt and allow the beans to cool
in the pot for 1 hour. Drain the beans,
saving at least 1/3 cup (80 ml) cooking
liquid. Discard the bay leaf.

Place the chickpeas in a food processor.
Add the garlic, lemon juice, tahini, and
1/3 cup (80 ml) reserved cooking liquid.
Purée until smooth, about 3 minutes.
Check the consistency of the hummus.
Do you like the texture, or is it too thick?
If it's too thick, add more bean liquid,
1 tablespoon (15 ml) at a time. Finally,
with the motor running, drizzle in the
olive oil and continue to purée until
it is fully incorporated.

Taste the hummus and add a little extra
sea salt if desired. Garnish with a drizzle
of olive oil and minced parsley. Serve
with tortilla chips *(see page 162)*, pita chips
(see page 152), or vegetables.

Note: Although I prefer the texture
of chickpeas that I cook myself, you can
substitute canned chickpeas for this recipe.
Use two 15-ounce (425 g) cans of chickpeas, rinsed and drained (reserve 1/3 cup
[80 ml] bean liquid for the hummus) and
cut back on or eliminate the salt. Canned
beans are pretty salty.

**Variations: Roasted Red Pepper
Hummus**—Add 1/4 cup (45 g) diced
roasted red pepper when puréeing the
hummus. Then add 2 tablespoons (22 g)
diced roasted red pepper to the top
of the finished hummus as a garnish.

Roasted Garlic Hummus—Omit the 2 cloves of fresh garlic and substitute 6 cloves of roasted garlic *(see page 166)* while puréeing. Roasted garlic is sweeter and more mellow than fresh, so you can add more without overpowering the dish. If you'd like, mince a couple more roasted cloves to use as a garnish on top of the finished hummus.

Tapenade Hummus—Mix 2 tablespoons (16 g) tapenade into the finished hummus. Stir to combine. Garnish the top with an additional tablespoon (8 g) of tapenade along with a drizzle of olive oil.

TIP: Adding a little baking soda when soaking dried beans helps soften the skin of the bean and speed the cooking process.

BABA GHANOUSH

I'm a fiend for eggplant. I even crave it sometimes.
Once you try this dip, I know you'll feel the same.

Yield: About 2 cups (450 g)

Ingredients

2 medium-size Italian eggplants,
    about 1 1/2 pounds (680 g) each

3 to 4 tablespoons (45 to 60 ml)
    extra-virgin olive oil, plus 1 teaspoon
    or so for garnish

1 teaspoon coarse sea salt or kosher salt,
    plus extra for sprinkling

1/2 cup (90 g) seeded and diced
    tomatoes, divided

2 tablespoons (30 g) tahini *(see page 53)*

2 tablespoons (28 ml) freshly
    squeeze lemon juice

1 teaspoon garlic purée *(see page 17)*
    or 2 cloves garlic, minced

1/2 teaspoon ground cumin

1 teaspoon minced fresh parsley *(see page 14)*,
    for garnish *(optional)*

Directions

Preheat the oven to 400ºF (200ºC,
or gas mark 6).

Slice the eggplants in half, lengthwise.
Prick the skin with a fork. Brush the
entire eggplant liberally with the olive
oil. Sprinkle the cut-side with some salt.
Place cut-side down on a baking sheet.
Place the baking sheet in the oven and
roast until the eggplant is soft, about
35 to 45 minutes. Remove the eggplant
from the oven. Tent loosely with aluminum
foil and allow to cool to room temperature.

Scrape the seeds from the cooled eggplant.
You don't have to remove all of them, just
try to get most. (The seeds can be a little
bitter.) Scrape the remaining eggplant
pulp into a food processor. Pulse 2 or 3
times to pulverize. Add 1/4 cup (45 g) of the
tomatoes, tahini, lemon juice, 1 teaspoon
salt, garlic, and cumin. Purée for 10 to 20
seconds to combine—the longer you
process, the smoother the dip.

Scrape into a serving bowl. Taste to see
if you'd like to add more salt. Top with
the remaining 1/4 cup (45 g) tomatoes.
Drizzle with the remaining 1 teaspoon
olive oil and sprinkle with the parsley.

Baba ghanoush is typically served with
warm pita bread, but you can also serve
it with pita chips *(see page 152)*, tortilla chips
(see page 162), or cucumber slices. It's good
at room temperature or chilled. Leftovers
can be stored, covered, in the refrigerated
for up to 5 days.

Note: Baba ghanoush can be lumpy or
smooth, your choice. If you prefer a little
more texture, you can mash the eggplant
pulp by hand with a fork and simply stir
in the other ingredients.

MOROCCAN-SPICED BEAN DIP

I was inspired to create this bean dip after tasting a Moroccan fava bean dip called bessara. If you like hummus, you'll love this flavorful dip! It's wonderful warm or cold.

Yield: 2 cups (450 g)

Ingredients

2 cans (14 ounces, or 390 g each) white kidney beans or butter beans *(see Note)*

1 clove garlic or 1/4 teaspoon garlic powder

3 tablespoons (45 ml) extra-virgin olive oil, plus extra for garnish

2 tablespoons (28 ml) lemon juice

1/2 teaspoon salt

3/4 teaspoon ground cumin, plus extra for garnish

1/4 teaspoon paprika, plus extra for garnish

1/8 teaspoon cayenne pepper, or more to taste

1 teaspoon minced fresh parsley *(see page 14)*, for garnish *(optional)*

Directions

Pour the beans, including their liquid, into a medium-size saucepan. Warm over medium heat until the beans are thoroughly heated, about 10 minutes. Drain the beans, reserving the liquid.

Transfer the beans to a food processor and add the garlic, olive oil, lemon juice, 2 tablespoons (28 ml) of the reserved liquid, and the spices. Process on high speed until smooth, adding more liquid if necessary to thin. The dip should be about the same thickness as hummus or refried beans. Taste the dip and adjust the seasonings if desired.

Garnish with ground cumin, paprika, olive oil, and/or minced parsley. Serve warm with pita chips *(see page 152)*, tortilla chips *(see page 162)*, or vegetables.

Note: You can substitute dried beans for this recipe. I love using Corona beans, a broad white bean that resembles a lima bean, but any white bean will do. Use 2/3 cup (167 g) dried beans. Soak overnight in cold water. Drain the soaking water from the beans. Put the soaked beans into a medium-size saucepan and cover completely with water by at least 1 inch (2.5 cm). Add 1 bay leaf, 2 cloves garlic, and a pinch of dried thyme. Bring to a boil over high heat. Reduce the heat and simmer until the beans are tender, 60 to 90 minutes, depending on the size of the beans. When the beans have softened, turn off the heat and add about 1/2 teaspoon sea salt or kosher salt. Allow the beans to cool at room temperature for 1 hour and then follow the recipe above.

TORTILLA CHIPS

These tortilla chips are very rustic. These are more like the chips that you might eat in Mexico—hearty, corn-flavored totopos. Compare them to a store-bought chip and you'll be blown away by the flavor.

Yield: 72 chips

Ingredients

2 cups (232 g) masa harina

1/4 teaspoon coarse sea salt or kosher salt, plus more sea salt for sprinkling

1 1/4 to 1 1/2 cups (295 to 355 ml) warm water

About 8 cups (1.9 L) rice bran, canola oil, or lard, for frying

Directions

Put the masa harina and 1/4 teaspoon salt in a medium-size mixing bowl and begin adding the water slowly, stirring constantly, until the dough is pliable but not sticky. The texture should be like pie crust. You should be able to roll it into a ball.

Knead the dough until it is well blended and evenly moistened, about 2 to 3 minutes. If the dough cracks while kneading, add a little more water. Cover the bowl with a damp towel and let stand for 10 minutes at room temperature.

Next, divide the dough into 12 equal balls, 1 1/2 inches (3.8 cm) in diameter, about the size of golf balls. Cover the balls with a towel again and let them rest for another 5 minutes.

In the meantime, preheat a large, ungreased cast-iron skillet or griddle over medium-high heat.

One at a time, place a ball between two layers of plastic wrap or waxed paper and flatten using a tortilla press or heavy skillet. I use a tortilla press because it's quick and gives you an even thickness, but you can definitely use a skillet instead. The finished tortilla should be very thin, no more than 1/8 inch (3 mm) thick, and about 5 inches (13 cm) wide. Peel the tortilla away from the plastic wrap carefully so it doesn't tear.

Place the pressed tortillas onto the ungreased griddle and cook between 45 seconds and 1 minute on one side and then flip to the other. Cook for an additional 45 seconds to 1 minute. When the tortilla starts to puff up, remove it from the pan. I cook the tortillas as I press them, instead of pressing them all and then cooking them. That way, the tortillas don't dry out.

Allow the tortillas to cool slightly. When they are cool enough to handle, cut them into 6 wedges each. Spread the wedges out onto baking sheets or a clean counter and cover with dry kitchen towels. Allow to air-dry for at least 2 hours. Sometimes I allow my chips to dry overnight. The drier

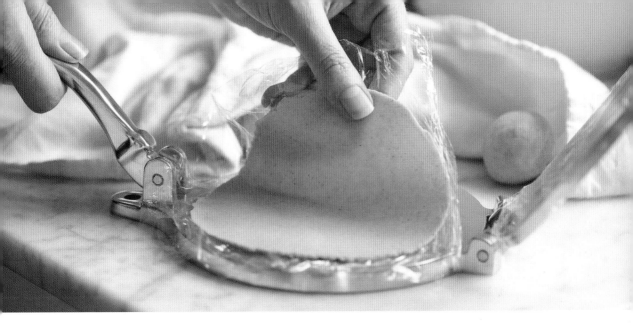

the tortillas, the crispier the final chips. Make sure they remain covered while drying so that they don't curl at the edges.

Next, heat the oil in a deep fryer or heavy-bottomed pan to 375ºF (190ºC). Line baking sheets with paper towels or brown paper bags for draining the chips.

Working in batches, fry the chips until just golden, about 5 minutes. They will continue to brown a bit even after you remove them from the oil, so don't over-brown them. Drain the chips on paper towels and sprinkle generously and immediately with salt.

Continue to fry the remaining chips. As you need space on the paper towels, transfer the finished chips to a bowl or a baking sheet in a warm oven (175º to 200ºF [79º to 93ºC]) until all the chips are fried. The chips can remain in the oven for up to 30 minutes.

Because of their thickness, these chips have a tendency to get soft when you try to store them. I recommend eating them within a few hours of making them for the best flavor and texture.

Note: Do not substitute corn flour or cornmeal for masa harina because they are made by a different process. Masa harina, also called masa de harina, is available online or in the Mexican food section of your grocery store. If you have a Mexican mercado in your area, it may sell fresh masa (premixed dough) by the pound, which can be substituted in place of the masa harina and water.

What Is Masa Harina?

Masa harina is a finely ground flour made from dried field corn that has been treated with a lime and water solution. It's a traditional ingredient in Mexican cooking and is used for tamales, tortillas, and sopas.

TOMATILLO SALSA

The flavor of tomatillos is bright and citrusy—a natural companion to a salty tortilla chip. I prefer them roasted because the process adds a subtle sweetness to the tang.

Yield: 3 cups (780 g)

Ingredients

1 pound (455 g) fresh tomatillos *(see page 143)*

1 or 2 fresh jalapeños or serrano chiles

1 plum tomato, coarsely chopped

1 or 2 cloves garlic, coarsely chopped

1 teaspoon sea salt or kosher salt

1/4 teaspoon ground cumin

3 tablespoons (30 g) minced white onion

2 tablespoons (2 g) minced cilantro

Directions

Preheat the broiler on high.

Remove the husks and stems from the tomatillos and rinse under cold water for a minute or so to remove the sticky residue.

Place the tomatillos stem-side down on an ungreased rimmed baking sheet. I place them stem-side down first so that they don't roll around when I am moving the baking sheet. Place the baking sheet 4 to 6 inches (10 to 15 cm) from the broiler. Broil for 5 minutes or until the tomatillos are beginning to char and blacken.

Remove the baking sheet from the oven and using tongs, turn the tomatillos over. Return them to the broiler until the second side has begun to char and blacken too, about 3 to 5 minutes. Remove the baking sheet from the oven and place it on a wire rack to cool.

In the meantime, place the chiles on a cutting board. I suggest using latex gloves to avoid irritating your skin when working with chiles. Use a paring knife to trim off the stem end. Then slice through the chiles lengthwise and open them on the cutting board. Use your paring knife to scrape away the seeds and ribs of the chiles. Discard. Chop the chiles coarsely. Place the chopped chiles in a food processor.

Using a rubber spatula, scrape the cooled tomatillos and any juice that accumulated while they cooled into the food processor as well. Add the tomato, garlic, salt, and cumin. Process until relatively smooth, about 1 minute.

Place the minced onion in a fine-mesh strainer and rinse under running water for 1 to 2 minutes. Shake to remove excess water and stir into the salsa, along with the cilantro. Taste to adjust the seasoning, if desired. Serve immediately or cover and refrigerate for up to 5 days.

How to Use Tomatillos

You may have walked by tomatillos in your grocery store and thought, "What are those things?" If you've never made your own salsa or chile verde, chances are you haven't purchased them. The loose papery husk that covers the fruit gives them the appearance of miniature Chinese paper lanterns. When the husk is peeled back, the fruit looks like a small green tomato.

Tomatillos are a relative of the tomato, with both belonging to the nightshade family along with chiles, potatoes, and eggplant. They are a great source of vitamins A and C.

The fruit is a bit sticky when the husk is peeled away, so they should be rinsed. Although you can use tomatillos raw in salads and salsas, they can be quite acidic. Roasting or boiling the fruit brings out a sweeter flavor and mellows the acidity a bit.

When purchasing tomatillos, choose small plum- or walnut-size fruit with dry, snug-fitting husks. The larger the fruit, the less intense the flavor. You can store them in their husks in the refrigerator for up to 1 month.

ROASTED TOMATO SALSA

Roasting the tomatoes helps enhance the natural sweetness, so you don't need the ripest summer tomatoes for success. However, if it's tomato season, you can make this recipe using fresh diced tomatoes instead of roasting them.

Yield: About 2 cups (520 g)

Ingredients

1 pound (455 g) ripe plum tomatoes, halved

1 large fresh jalapeño chile or serrano chile

3 cloves garlic, unpeeled

1 teaspoon coarse sea salt or kosher salt

1/4 cup (40 g) finely diced white onion

1/4 to 1/2 cup (4 to 8 g) chopped cilantro *(optional)*

1 1/2 teaspoons lime juice

Directions

Preheat the broiler on high.

Lay the tomatoes on a rimmed baking sheet and place about 4 to 6 inches (10 to 15 cm) from the broiler. Roast until charred and blackened on one side, about 6 minutes. Using tongs, turn the tomatoes over and roast on the other side until slightly blackened. Remove from the oven and let cool on the baking sheet on a wire rack.

Meanwhile, line a cast-iron skillet or griddle with heavy-duty aluminum foil. Preheat the skillet over medium-high heat for 5 minutes. Place the chile and unpeeled garlic into the preheated skillet. Roast, turning occasionally, until the chile and garlic are blackened in spots and soft, 10 to 15 minutes. Remove them from the pan and allow to rest until cool enough to handle.

Slice the chile lengthwise to expose the seeds. Use a paring knife to scrape out the seeds and ribs. It's always a good idea to wear plastic or latex gloves when you are working with chiles.

When the garlic has cooled, peel the papery skin from each clove.

Place the chile and garlic in a food processor along with the salt and grind the mixture into a coarse paste. Stop to scrape down the sides of the bowl once or twice. Add the tomatoes and any juices that have accumulated on the baking sheet and pulse a few times until you have a coarse-textured purée. Transfer the salsa to a serving bowl.

Place the diced onion in a fine-mesh strainer and rinse the onion under running water for 1 to 2 minutes. Shake to remove excess water and stir into the salsa, along with the cilantro and lime juice. Taste and season with additional salt, if desired.

This salsa is great at room temperature or chilled. If you prefer it cold, refrigerate it for at least 1 hour prior to serving. For best flavor, eat within a day or two of making.

GUACAMOLE

When it comes to guacamole, I'm conflicted. On one hand, I love a good chunky guacamole like guacamole naranja (chunky guacamole with orange juice). On the other hand, sometimes I just crave smooth, rich avocado. My go-to guacamole is pretty simple, as you'll see, but it really hits the spot!

Yield: About 2 cups (450 g)

Ingredients

3 medium-size Hass avocados

1 tablespoon (15 ml) lemon juice
   or 4 teaspoons (20 ml) lime juice

3/4 teaspoon sea salt or kosher salt,
   or more to taste

1/2 teaspoon garlic purée *(see page 17)*
   or 1/8 teaspoon garlic powder

3 dashes original or jalapeño Tabasco
   sauce, or more to taste

Directions

Starting at the stem end, slice down through the tip of the avocado to the pit. When your knife hits the pit, begin to turn the avocado counterclockwise until you've gone all the way around it and end up where you started. Remove the blade and twist the avocado to separate the two halves. The pit will remain in one half. Place the half with the pit on a cutting board with the pit facing up. Being careful not to cut yourself, chop into the pit with your knife. Twist the knife to loosen the pit from the flesh. Tap the handle of the knife over a garbage can or compost container to dislodge the pit. Repeat with the remaining 2 avocados.

Use a large kitchen spoon to scoop the flesh from the skin into a medium-size mixing bowl. Mash the flesh with a potato masher or fork to the desired consistency. I like mine relatively smooth, but you can leave it chunky instead. Add the juice, salt, garlic, and Tabasco sauce. Stir to blend. Taste to see if you'd like to add more seasoning.

Serve with tortilla chips *(see page 162)* or jicama sticks sprinkled with chile powder and lime juice.

How to Select Hass Avocado

When selecting Hass avocados, try to pick fruit with dark green, almost purple skin. The avocado should give slightly when you apply pressure, but if it's really soft, it is probably bruised or overripe.

If your market doesn't have ripe avocados, you can buy firm green ones and ripen them at home. The quickest way to ripen an avocado is to place it in a paper bag, fold the top of the bag over to close it, and leave it on the counter for a couple of days.

GUACAMOLE NARANJA

On a trip to San Antonio, Texas, my husband and I were walking along the Riverwalk when we passed a cafe. A waiter with a cart full of ingredients was chopping an avocado into a bowl of fruit juice—tableside guacamole. I was sold!

Yield: 1 1/2 cups (338 g)

Ingredients

1/4 cup (60 ml) freshly squeezed orange juice

2 tablespoons (28 ml) freshly squeezed lime juice

1/2 teaspoon salt

1 large or 2 medium avocados

2 Roma tomatoes, roasted, peeled, seeded, and diced *(see sidebar)*

1/2 to 1 serrano chile, roasted, seeded, and minced *(see sidebar)*

1/4 cup (40 g) diced red onion

1/4 cup (4 g) chopped fresh cilantro

Directions

Combine the orange juice, lime juice, and salt in a medium-size bowl. Stir until the salt is fully dissolved. Halve the avocado(s). Remove the pit and scoop the flesh into the salted juice. Use 2 butter knives to ruggedly chop the avocado. This guacamole is rustic, so don't worry about precise cuts.

Next, stir in the diced tomatoes and chile. Add a little chile at a time so that you get just the right amount of heat. Then add the red onion and cilantro and stir to blend. Serve with tortilla chips *(see page 162)* and a frosty margarita!

TIP: Roasting Tomatoes and Chiles

Line a cast-iron or heavy sauté pan with aluminum foil. Heat the pan over medium-high heat. Add the tomatoes and chiles to the pan. Use tongs to turn often until they are charred on all sides and starting to soften, 8 to 10 minutes. Remove from the pan and let cool. When the tomatoes are cool enough to handle, peel away most of the charred skin using a sharp paring knife. Then, slice the tomatoes in half lengthwise, scoop out the seeds, and dice. When the chiles are cool, slice in half lengthwise and use the tip of your paring knife to scrape out the seeds and ribs. Mince.

RESOURCES

Chefshop.com
Quality artisan foods from around
the world, including traditionally
made vinegar, olive oil, rice bran oil,
and much more

www.chefshop.com
800-596-0885

Penzeys Spices
Dried herbs and spices

www.penzeys.com
800-741-7787

Seattle Fish Company
Fresh fish (including fish bones) and
shellfish, from the docks to your door

www.seattlefishcompany.com
866-938-7576

Slab Art Studios
Original artisan furniture, including
dining tables, natural cutting boards,
and art objects from locally salvaged trees

www.slabart.com
206-412-8658

About the Author

Erin Coopey is a chef, writer, and food photographer in Seattle, Washington. After receiving her culinary degree in Scottsdale, Arizona, Erin trained at the prestigious Culinary Institute of America at Greystone. Her love of food has many facets from recipe development to food photography and catering to teaching.

Erin's recipes have appeared in numerous publications, including *Good Morning America's Cut the Calories Cookbook*, edited by Jean Anderson and Sara Moulton, KAET Channel 8's cookbook series including *I Is for International* and *E Is for Entertaining*, SheSpeaks.com, and Yahoo! Shine. Erin has appeared on several television programs to demonstrate recipes and products.

Her great passion is teaching, having taught hundreds of students over the past twenty years.

She currently teaches throughout the Puget Sound with South Seattle Community College, PCC Natural Markets, Chefshop.com, and Parties That Cook, and privately through The Glorified HomeChef.

INDEX

Also Available

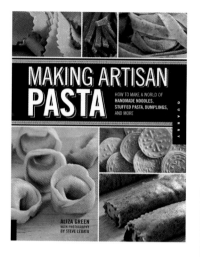

Making Artisan Pasta

978-1-59253-732-7

Real Food Fermentation

978-1-59253-784-6

Cheesemaker's Apprentice

978-1-59253-755-6

Homegrown Sprouts

978-1-59253-870-6

The Soupmaker's Kitchen

978-1-59253-844-7